THE TRANSGENDER
STORIES OF RESILIENCE AND TRIUMPH

Ajit Kumar

The Transgender Stories of Resilience & Triumph

The Transgender Stories of Resilience & Triumph

Ajit Kumar

Published by Ajit Kumar, 2024.

While every precaution has been taken in the preparation of this book, the publisher assumes no responsibility for errors or omissions, or for damages resulting from the use of the information contained herein.

THE TRANSGENDER STORIES OF RESILIENCE & TRIUMPH

First edition. January 14, 2024.

ISBN: 979-8224070084

Written by Ajit Kumar.

Disclaimer:

"The stories of this book are entirely based on the real life incidences who set mile stones by their acts."

e-mail: ajitjha0904@gmail.com

Table of Contents

Acknowledgement

Writing this book wasn't just about crafting words on a page; it was weaving together the vibrant threads of resilience, self-discovery, and unwavering dreams. It was a testament to the extraordinary journeys of transgender individuals who dared to carve their own paths in a world that often tries to confine them.

To the incredible souls who shared their stories on various platforms such as TV Shows, articles in the news-paper and through their inspired work. My deepest gratitude to them to be a vulnerable and work what you love the most. Your words became the beating heart of this book, and your courage continues to inspire me every day. Writing about Transgender's and about their stories since my first article when I encountered with a transgender on a road and listened her story. I wrote article on that in 2021. That was just reflection but from that time I started to think about it and started to collect data of transgenders from internet sources.

Firstly, my heartfelt thanks to the almighty because without almighty's grace, I won't do anything. After that my family who always stood with me and motivates me to write. Even, they told me to sleep in late night because I worked in an office every day and after that I work on my own projects like this. They are always concern about my health and peace. Special thanks to my elder brother Surjeet and sister-in-law - Nisha who everyday ask me about this book and this statement motivates me to complete.

My deepest gratitude to Himanshu, whose artistic hand crafted the perfect cover page for this book. His expertise was invaluable, transforming my vision into a tangible masterpiece that wouldn't exist without his generosity.My sincere thanks to Manisha who proof read my few chapters and provide me valuable feedback to this work. Rashmi Gosain's unwavering curiosity about the book wasn't just a nudge, it was a warm ember that kept my creative fire stoked. For that,

I'll forever be indebted to her guiding light.I owe special thanks to Gunjan and Sunil, an amazing friend whose insights proved invaluable during the manuscript preparation.

My heart overflows with gratitude for my forever friends Prashant, Sunita, Shivam, Nishi, Surbhi, Chandrapal Raj, Sarita, Azazul, Simrat, Khuloos and Somya your unwavering support through thick and thin means the world to me. Distance hasn't dimmed the warm glow of love and trust I share with former colleagues Dhruv, Naveen, and Shiv. Their bond remains a cherished treasure.

To the invaluable team who helped shape this manuscript, my deepest respect to the publisher who provide me a platform to showcase my work in front of the society and literary world. To the community that held me up and pushed me forward, my eternal gratitude. Transgender authors, activists, and everyone who has fought for a world where we can all exist freely – your voices echoed in every chapter, reminding me of the power of collective action.

And most importantly, to the readers who pick up this book, my deepest hope. May you find solace in these stories, inspiration in the face of adversity, and a renewed belief in the power of the human spirit. This book is a celebration of individuality, a call to embrace our unique identities, and a reminder that we are all capable of creating a world where everyone can thrive.

Thank you for being a part of this journey.

01. Echoes of Resilience: Amplifying Transgender Voices

Padmini Prakash, a beacon of vibrant resilience in a tapestry of diverse identities, is a name etched in the annals of LGBTQIA+ activism in India. Her journey, traversing societal challenges and personal triumphs, resonates as a powerful testament to the indomitable spirit of the transgender community. Born into a conservative background in Tamil Nadu, Padmini's earliest struggles stemmed from the dissonance between her inner identity and the expectations thrust upon her as a male-assigned child. Despite societal pressures and familial anxieties, she embraced her true self, transitioning at the age of 16.

Facing a world steeped in prejudice and discrimination, Padmini refused to be subjugated. She donned the mantle of an activist, her voice ringing out against archaic norms and advocating for the rights of her community. In the early 2000s, she co-founded the Transgender Resource Centre (TRC), a haven for ostracized individuals seeking acceptance and support. The TRC transcended being a mere organization; it became a vibrant community center, offering counselling, legal aid, and educational opportunities, empowering individuals to rise above societal barriers.

Padmini's activism extended beyond the confines of the TRC. She tirelessly lobbied for equal rights, traversing the corridors of power and engaging in dialogues with lawmakers. Her relentless pursuit of the Transgender Persons (Protection of Rights) Bill was instrumental in its eventual passage in 2019, a landmark achievement that granted legal recognition and basic rights to the transgender community.But Padmini's impact transcends policy frameworks. She is a storyteller, weaving narratives of resilience and hope through her memoir, 'Landmarks: The Memoirs of a Transgender Woman'. Her powerful words challenge stereotypes, fostering empathy and understanding in the hearts of readers. She is an educator, dispelling myths and raising awareness about transgender issues through workshops and public speaking engagements.

Padmini is also a performer, harnessing the power of art to dismantle prejudice. Her vibrant Bharatanatyam performances, defying traditional gender roles, redefine the boundaries of the art form while simultaneously challenging societal narratives. Through her expressive movements, she paints a portrait of grace and defiance, challenging societal perceptions and asserting the right to celebrate her identity on her own terms.

Perhaps the most significant aspect of Padmini's legacy is her unwavering belief in the potential of her community. She fosters a spirit of self-reliance and entrepreneurship, encouraging members to carve their own destinies. Her work with the Transgender Unity Trust, providing microloans and skill development training, empowers individuals to build sustainable livelihoods and challenge economic vulnerability.

Padmini Prakash's story is not merely a personal narrative; it is a collective tapestry woven with threads of struggle, resilience, and relentless pursuit of justice. Her life and work stand as a testament to the indomitable spirit of the transgender community, reminding us that true change and acceptance come from collective understanding and unwavering advocacy. As Padmini continues to champion the rights of her community, her voice echoes a message of hope, urging us to embrace diversity and build a world where every individual can thrive, regardless of their assigned gender at birth.

02. From Pradeep to Prithika: A Portrait of Transgender Triumph

K. Prithika Yashini, born Pradeep Kumar, is a name synonymous with courage and resilience. Her story, etched in the annals of India's LGBTQIA+ history, is not just a personal triumph, but a testament to the unwavering spirit of the transgender community in the face of discrimination and systemic hurdles.

Hailing from a modest background in Tamil Nadu, Prithika's childhood was marked by an uncomfortable dissonance between her assigned gender and her true identity. Despite societal pressures and familial anxieties, she embraced her womanhood at the age of 19, undergoing gender reassignment surgery. However, her journey was far from over.

Facing a world steeped in prejudice, Prithika refused to be defined by limitations. She dreamt of serving her community, not just as a member, but as a protector. Driven by an unwavering determination, she set her sights on joining the Tamil Nadu police force.But the path to becoming a police officer was fraught with challenges. The application form offered only two options: male or female. Prithika, undeterred, challenged the archaic binary system, marking her application as "transgender." This bold move was met with resistance. Her application was initially rejected, citing technicalities and societal norms.

Prithika, however, was not one to back down. She embarked on a legal battle, her tenacity resonating with the spirit of the Supreme Court's NALSA judgment recognizing the "third gender." After facing numerous hurdles and enduring discriminatory remarks, she finally emerged victorious. In 2017, she made history, becoming the first transgender woman to be appointed a police officer in Tamil Nadu.But Prithika's impact transcends her appointment. She stands as a beacon of hope, inspiring countless transgender individuals to dream beyond societal expectations. Her story, documented in the film "Breaking the Code," serves as a powerful reminder that one's identity cannot be a barrier to success.

Her dedication extends beyond the uniform. Prithika actively champions the rights of her community, using her platform to advocate for inclusivity and acceptance. She mentors aspiring transgender officers, sharing her experiences and guiding them through the bureaucratic maze. She tirelessly combats discrimination, challenging discriminatory practices and policies within the police force itself.

Furthermore, Prithika is a voice for change beyond the confines of law enforcement. She participates in public forums, engages with diverse communities, and spearheads awareness campaigns, dismantling prejudice brick by brick. Her powerful narrative challenges stereotypes and fosters empathy, paving the way for a more understanding and inclusive society.

K. Prithika Yashini's story is more than just a personal victory; it is a testament to the unwavering spirit of the transgender community. Her journey speaks of resilience, defiance, and a relentless pursuit of justice. As she continues to champion equality and acceptance, Prithika stands as a symbol of hope, reminding us that even the most formidable brass ceilings can be shattered with courage, determination, and unwavering belief in oneself.

03 Blooming Beyond Walls: Journey of Blossoming

With a radiant smile and unwavering spirit, Dr. Manabi Bandopadhyay stands tall as a beacon of hope for the transgender community in India. Her life, a tapestry woven with threads of perseverance, defiance, and profound achievements, offers a testament to the boundless potential of an individual fuelled by an unyielding quest for acceptance and equality.

Born Somnath Banerjee in West Bengal, Manabi's early years were marked by a constant dissonance between her assigned gender and her inner identity. Facing societal pressures and taunts from loved ones, she embraced her womanhood at the age of 23, undergoing gender-affirming surgery in 2003. This courageous decision paved the way for a new chapter, marked by both personal and professional triumphs.

Driven by a thirst for knowledge, Manabi pursued her academic aspirations with a single-minded focus. She completed her Master's degree in Bengali and then became the first transgender individual from West Bengal to earn a Ph.D. This academic excellence, coupled with her innate leadership qualities, led her to the helm of Krishnagar Women's College in 2015, shattering glass ceilings and becoming the first openly transgender principal in India.However, Manabi's impact extends far beyond the four walls of academia. She is a fierce advocate for the transgender community, tirelessly raising her voice against discrimination and advocating for equal rights. Her journey led her to the Bigg Boss Bangla reality show in 2013, where she used the platform to educate audiences about the challenges faced by transgender individuals and dispel harmful stereotypes.

Manabi's activism also finds expression in her artistic pursuits. She made her acting debut in the film "Purba Paschim Dakshin," using the medium of cinema to tell stories that resonate with the lived experiences of the transgender community and challenge societal perceptions.But perhaps her most inspiring contribution is the establishment of the Manabi Bandopadhyay Trust, an organization dedicated to empowering transgender individuals through education, skill development, and social welfare initiatives. Through this venture, Manabi champions economic independence and provides vital support to members of her community who often face marginalization and unemployment.

Dr. Manabi Bandopadhyay's life is a powerful reminder that the human spirit can persevere amidst adversity. She is a role model, a leader, and a voice of hope for countless individuals navigating the complexities of gender identity. Her journey proves that with unwavering determination, one can not only break down barriers but also pave the way for a more inclusive and just society.As Manabi continues to champion the rights of the transgender community, her story resonates as a clarion call for acceptance, understanding, and equal opportunities. Her legacy is a testament to the transformative power of individual courage and the boundless potential that lies within us all when we embrace our true selves.

04 A Fierce Spirit Paving the Way for Change

Laxmi Narayan Tripathi, often simply known as Laxmi, is a name synonymous with activism, grace, and resilience in the Indian transgender community. Her journey, etched in the annals of LGBTQIA+ history, is a vibrant tapestry woven with personal triumphs, fierce advocacy, and a relentless pursuit of equality.

Born in Mumbai in 1978, Laxmi's early life was marked by societal pressures and the dissonance between her assigned gender and her true identity. At the age of five, she knew she was different, drawn to feminine ways despite identifying as male. However, facing a world steeped in prejudice, she found solace in the hijra community, a traditional transgender group in India.

Embracing her true self, Laxmi underwent gender-affirming surgery at the age of 16. But her journey was far from over. Facing discrimination, social ostracization, and limited opportunities, she channelled her challenges into strength. She honed her skills as a Bharatanatyam dancer, dazzling audiences with her grace and defying traditional gender norms in the art form. Her talents caught the eye of filmmakers, leading her to roles in Bollywood movies and television shows. Her on-screen presence not only challenged stereotypes but also provided crucial visibility for the transgender community. However, Laxmi's true calling lay in activism. Recognizing the plight of many transgender individuals who faced discrimination and violence, she co-founded the "Sai Trinity Foundation," an organization dedicated to providing education, healthcare, and social support to the community.

Laxmi's advocacy extended beyond her foundation. She actively campaigned for legal rights and recognition for transgender individuals, tirelessly lobbying the government and raising awareness through public speaking engagements. Her fierce spirit and eloquent voice resonated with many, garnering her international recognition and a platform to address the United Nations in 2008. In 2019, Laxmi's efforts bore fruit when the Indian government passed the Transgender Persons (Protection of Rights) Bill, granting legal recognition and basic rights to the community. This landmark achievement was a direct result of her relentless advocacy and the tireless efforts of numerous activists.

But Laxmi's fight continues. She works to dismantle discriminatory practices, advocating for equal access to education, employment, and healthcare. She empowers transgender individuals to pursue their dreams and fight for their rightful place in society.Beyond activism, Laxmi is a celebrated writer and motivational speaker. Her autobiography, "Me Hijra, Me Laxmi," offers a poignant glimpse into her life and struggles, while her motivational talks inspire individuals to embrace their identities and overcome adversity.

Laxmi Narayan Tripathi's story is a testament to the unyielding spirit of the human heart. It is a story of defying limitations, overcoming prejudice, and paving the way for a more inclusive world. Her journey continues to inspire countless individuals, reminding us that one voice, especially when amplified with such resilience and determination, can truly make a difference. Her legacy goes beyond personal achievements. She stands as a beacon of hope, a fierce advocate, and a champion for equality. As she continues to fight for the rights of her community, her voice echoes a message of acceptance and understanding, urging us to build a world where every individual can thrive, regardless of their gender identity.

05. Journey from Margin to Mainstream

Joyita Mondal's life paints a vivid portrait of resilience and triumph against a backdrop of societal challenges. Born in a small village in West Bengal, India, Joyita's journey as a transgender woman is woven with threads of self-acceptance, unwavering activism, and a relentless pursuit of equality for her community.

From a young age, Joyita felt a dissonance between her assigned gender and her inner reality. Despite societal pressures and limited understanding, she embraced her true identity at the age of 19. This courageous decision, however, marked the beginning of a long and arduous battle against discrimination and marginalization.Facing ostracization and economic hardship, Joyita refused to be defined by limitations. She honed her tailoring skills, her nimble fingers weaving not just garments, but a path towards self-reliance. Her talent and determination soon blossomed into a thriving tailoring business, providing not just a livelihood but also a space of empowerment for other transgender individuals.

Beyond her personal success, Joyita's heart yearned for a more inclusive society. Witnessing the struggles of her community, she co-founded the transgender rights organization "Gourab Srijani Sangha." This became a beacon of hope, offering support, legal aid, and vocational training to empower marginalized transgender individuals.Joyita's activism wasn't confined to local spaces. She became a vocal advocate on national platforms, raising awareness about the plight of the transgender community through interviews, public forums, and even reality TV shows. Her eloquent voice challenged discriminatory practices and outdated norms, urging for recognition and equal rights.

One of Joyita's most significant contributions was her pivotal role in securing legal recognition for transgender individuals in India. Her tireless efforts, alongside countless others, culminated in the landmark

Transgender Persons (Protection of Rights) Bill of 2019, granting basic rights and legal protection to the community.However, Joyita's fight for equality continues. She recognizes the need for sustained efforts to dismantle systemic discrimination and ensure access to education, healthcare, and employment opportunities for transgender individuals. Her organization continues to provide crucial support and resources, fostering a sense of community and belonging.

Joyita Mondal's story is not just a personal narrative; it is a testament to the collective spirit of the transgender community. Her journey signifies the power of self-acceptance, the unwavering pursuit of justice, and the unwavering belief in a more equitable future. As she continues to champion the rights of her community, Joyita leaves a legacy of hope and inspiration, reminding us that even amidst adversity, the human spirit can soar with unwavering resilience.

06. Shattering Glass Ceilings - Paving the Way

Amidst the bustling halls of the Madras Bar Council in Chennai, Sathyasri Sharmila etched her name in history. In June 2018, she became India's first transgender lawyer, a milestone not just for herself, but for an entire community yearning for acceptance and equality. Her journey, fraught with challenges and fuelled by an unwavering spirit, exemplifies the transformative power of resilience and determination.

Born Udhakumar in a small village in Tamil Nadu, Sathyasri's childhood was marked by an internal dissonance between her assigned gender and her true identity. Growing up in a society steeped in societal pressures, she faced taunts and ostracization for expressing her feminine spirit. Yet, her yearning for self-acceptance was indomitable.

At the age of 23, Sathyasri made a life-altering decision - she underwent gender-affirming surgery. This courageous act, though liberating, was met with resistance from family and community. Despite the hardships, Sathyasri's resolve to carve her own path remained unwavering.Driven by a thirst for knowledge and a desire to empower her community, Sathyasri pursued her legal education. Years of relentless studying amidst societal prejudice culminated in a pivotal moment - her enrolment in the Bar Council. As she stood amidst 485 fellow graduates, ready to take the oath, a wave of emotions washed over her - pride, accomplishment, and a quiet defiance against the barriers she had shattered.

Sathyasri's appointment wasn't just a personal victory; it was a beacon of hope for the transgender community. Her success paved the way for greater inclusivity within the legal system and inspired countless individuals to pursue their dreams. It also ignited a fire within Sathyasri to be more than just a lawyer; she became a voice for the voiceless, a crusader for transgender rights.She actively participates in public forums, raising awareness about the challenges faced by the transgender community and advocating for policy changes. Her courtroom battles go beyond individual cases; they fight for systemic equality, challenging discriminatory practices and advocating for equal access to education, healthcare, and employment opportunities.

Sathyasri's story is not just about personal triumph; it's about dismantling prejudice, brick by brick. Through her legal expertise and unwavering spirit, she is building a more inclusive India, where gender identity is not a hurdle but a celebration of diversity.Sathyasri Sharmila's journey is far from over. As she continues to champion the rights of her community, her story serves as a powerful reminder that the human spirit can soar even in the face of adversity. She is a testament to the transformative power of courage, compassion, and the unwavering belief in a future where acceptance reigns supreme.

07. Crown of Courage - The Transqueen

In the dazzling world of pageantry, where shimmering gowns and sculpted physiques often define beauty, Nitasha Biswas carved a path of her own. Crowned Miss Transqueen India in 2017, she became the first transgender woman to hold the title, not only shattering glass ceilings but rewriting the very definition of beauty and grace.

Born as a boy in Kolkata, Nitasha's childhood was a tapestry woven with whispers and judgments. The dissonance between her assigned gender and her inner truth cast a long shadow, but her spirit remained undimmed. At the age of 26, she made the life-altering decision to undergo gender-affirming surgery, stepping into her authentic self with courage and conviction.However, societal hurdles awaited. Facing discrimination and limited opportunities, Nitasha refused to be confined by societal expectations. Fuelled by a hunger for success and a desire to empower her community, she pursued a Master's in Business Management, defying stereotypes and carving her own path.

The Miss Transqueen India pageant presented a unique platform for Nitasha. It wasn't just a showcase of beauty; it was a battle cry for inclusivity and acceptance. As she glided across the stage in her resplendent gown, her confidence and eloquence shone brighter than any diamond tiara. In that moment, she wasn't just competing for a crown; she was vying for a voice, a chance to change the narrative around transgender beauty and identity.

The judges saw the fire in Nitasha's eyes, the resilience in her smile, and the unwavering spirit that defined her being. The crown, when placed upon her head, wasn't just a symbol of victory; it was a beacon of hope for countless transgender individuals, a powerful message that beauty transcends societal norms and gender binaries.Beyond the glitz and glamour of the pageant, Nitasha used her platform to champion the rights of her community. She became a vocal advocate for legal recognition, equal opportunities, and an end to discrimination. She participated in public forums, sharing her story and the struggles faced by transgender individuals, urging for empathy and understanding.

Nitasha's impact extends far beyond raising awareness. She established the NGO "Queens of Kolkata," providing vocational training and financial assistance to marginalized transgender women. She also launched a talent management agency, opening doors for other aspiring transgender models and performers.Her journey hasn't been without its challenges. Nitasha faces prejudice and scepticism on a daily basis, but she navigates these hurdles with grace and fortitude. Her unwavering optimism and unyielding spirit serve as an inspiration to both the transgender community and society at large.

Nitasha Biswas's story is not just about a crown; it's about challenging paradigms, rewriting narratives, and paving the way for a more inclusive world. She stands as a testament to the power of self-acceptance, the boundless potential of human spirit, and the transformative beauty of breaking down barriers and embracing our true selves.

08. Building Bridges with Grace-Artistic Expression

In the vibrant tapestry of India's LGBTQIA+ community, Jiya Das stands out as a thread of resilience, woven with artistic expression and a tireless fight for inclusivity. Born Ashutosh in a small village in West Bengal, Jiya's journey is a poignant testament to the human spirit's unwavering pursuit of self-acceptance and the power of creativity to spark change.

From a young age, Jiya felt a dissonance between her assigned gender and her true identity. Facing societal pressures and limited understanding, she found solace in dance. The movement of her body, the way it expressed emotions unheard, became a refuge and a language that resonated beyond words. At the age of 19, Jiya made the life-altering decision to transition, embracing her womanhood with courage and grace.

However, societal hurdles awaited. Navigating discrimination and limited opportunities, Jiya refused to be confined by societal expectations. She honed her dancing skills, her nimble feet weaving tales of struggle and resilience through Bharatanatyam, a classical Indian dance form. Her performances, imbued with raw emotion and breathtaking fluidity, captivated audiences both in India and abroad.But Jiya's ambition went beyond captivating stages. She recognized the transformative power of art in dismantling prejudice and advocating for inclusivity. She founded the "Queens of Kolkata" dance troupe, a vibrant collective of transgender dancers who showcased their talent and stories on platforms previously inaccessible to them.

Through her captivating performances and workshops, Jiya challenged rigid notions of beauty and gender expression. She redefined the classical dance form, infusing it with modern elements and themes relevant to the transgender community. Her choreography became a powerful voice, shattering stereotypes and demanding acceptance.Beyond the stage, Jiya became a vocal advocate for transgender rights. She participated in public forums, sharing her experiences and urging for empathy and understanding. She actively collaborated with NGOs and government agencies, pushing for policy changes and better access to healthcare, education, and employment opportunities for her community.

Jiya's impact extends far beyond raising awareness. She established the "Transgender Art and Culture Academy," a space where individuals can learn and express themselves through various art forms. This initiative, a beacon of hope and empowerment, fosters talent and opens doors for aspiring transgender artists and performers.However, Jiya's journey hasn't been without its challenges. She faces prejudice and scepticism on a daily basis, yet she navigates these hurdles with steadfast optimism and unwavering spirit. Her message of resilience and defiance resonates with countless individuals within and beyond the LGBTQIA+ community.

More than just steps, Jiya Das's dance redefines narratives, builds bridges, and challenges norms. Her story isn't just about dance; it's about inclusivity, self-expression, and breaking barriers. With every move, she reminds us of the transformative power of art and the boundless potential of the human spirit.

09. A Beacon of Hope

Esther Bharathi's life pulsates with the vibrant rhythm of defiance and resilience. Born Manoj in a small village in Tamil Nadu, Esther's journey is a testament to the unwavering spirit of self-acceptance and the transformative power of pursuing one's dreams against all odds.

From a young age, Esther felt a dissonance between her assigned gender and her inner truth. Societal pressures and limited understanding cast a shadow on her childhood, but her spirit remained ignited by a yearning for self-expression. At the age of 25, she made the life-altering decision to undergo gender-affirming surgery, stepping into her authentic self with courage and grace.However, navigating societal prejudices was no easy feat. Discrimination and limited opportunities threatened to confine Esther, but her refusal to be defined by limitations proved formidable. She honed her tailoring skills, her nimble fingers weaving not just garments but self-reliance and a path towards empowering others.

Beyond personal success, Esther's heart yearned for a more inclusive society. Witnessing the struggles of her community, she co-founded the transgender rights organization "Gourab Srijani Sangha." This became a beacon of hope, offering support, legal aid, and vocational training to empower marginalized transgender individuals.Esther's activism resonated beyond local spaces. She became a vocal advocate on national platforms, raising awareness about the plight of the transgender community through interviews, public forums, and even reality TV shows. Her eloquent voice challenged discriminatory practices and outdated norms, urging for recognition and equal rights.

One of Esther's most significant contributions was her pivotal role in securing legal recognition for transgender individuals in India. Her tireless efforts, alongside countless others, culminated in the landmark Transgender Persons (Protection of Rights) Bill of 2019, granting basic rights and legal protection to the community.However, Esther's fight for equality continues. She recognizes the need for sustained efforts to dismantle systemic discrimination and ensure access to education, healthcare, and employment opportunities for transgender individuals. Her organization continues to provide crucial support and resources, fostering a sense of community and belonging.

More than just one voice, Esther Bharathi's story is a powerful anthem for the transgender community. Her life champions self-acceptance, relentless pursuit of justice, and unwavering belief in a fairer future. As she fights for her community's rights, Esther leaves a legacy of hope and inspiration, proving that even when shadows fall, the human spirit, fuelled by resilience and unity, can reach for the sky.

10. From Social Activist to Electoral Pioneer

In the vibrant tapestry of Indian democracy, a thread of courage and defiance shines particularly bright: Mumtaz. Not just a name, but a symbol of resilience and a beacon of hope for the transgender community, Mumtaz became the first transgender person to contest elections in Punjab in 2017. Her journey, etched with both struggle and triumph, is a testament to the unwavering spirit of self-acceptance and the transformative power of political participation.

Born into a Dalit family in rural Punjab, Mumtaz's childhood was marked by the double bind of societal prejudice – both for being transgender and belonging to a marginalized caste. Dreams were often overshadowed by whispers, opportunities restricted by discrimination. Yet, Mumtaz's spirit remained unyielding.

At the age of 23, she made the life-altering decision to undergo gender-affirming surgery. This courageous act, though liberating, came at a steep price. Ostracized by her family and ostracized by society, Mumtaz found solace in the Bahujan Samaj Party (BSP), a political party known for championing the rights of marginalized communities.For over a decade, Mumtaz worked tirelessly with the BSP, her gentle voice carrying the weight of countless unheard stories. She witnessed firsthand the struggles of her community, the systemic discrimination that denied them access to education, healthcare, and equal opportunities.

It was this fire within, this yearning for change, that led Mumtaz to take the unprecedented step of contesting the 2017 Punjab Assembly elections. Her chosen constituency, Bhucho Mandi, was a microcosm of the issues she passionately sought to address – poverty, unemployment, and rampant discrimination against marginalized communities.Her campaign was unlike any other. Gone were the posters with polished faces and grandiose promises. Mumtaz walked the dusty streets, knocking on doors, her voice hoarse from sharing her experiences and the struggles of her community. She spoke of equality, of dignity, of a future where identity wasn't a hurdle but a celebration.

While the electoral outcome wasn't a victory in the traditional sense, Mumtaz's impact transcended mere numbers. She shattered the glass ceiling, paving the way for increased political participation within the transgender community. Her campaign ignited a conversation, forcing society to confront its biases and acknowledge the voices that had been silenced for far too long.

Beyond the spotlight, Mumtaz continues her fight for equality. She works with various NGOs, advocating for legal recognition, access to education, and livelihood opportunities for transgender individuals. She sits on government panels, ensuring that policy decisions are informed by the lived experiences of her community.Mumtaz's story is not just about a single election; it's about a revolution that is still unfolding. Her unwavering courage, her relentless pursuit of justice, and her unwavering belief in the power of democratic participation have become a source of inspiration for countless individuals.

She stands as a testament to the fact that even amidst adversity, the human spirit can soar. Mumtaz's journey is far from over, but she has already etched her name in the annals of Indian history, not just as the first transgender candidate, but as a pioneer of change, a champion of equality, and a symbol of hope for a more inclusive and just future.

11. Beyond Representation Whispers to Victory

Shabnam Mausi's story is woven into the fabric of Indian history, a testament to unwavering resilience and the power of defying societal norms. In 2000, she shattered glass ceilings with a resounding thud, becoming the first transgender person in India to be elected as a Member of the Legislative Assembly (MLA). Her journey, however, is far from a singular triumph; it's a saga of hardship, self-acceptance, and a relentless pursuit of justice for the marginalized.

Born Ashutosh in a small village in Madhya Pradesh, Shabnam's childhood was defined by whispers and ostracization. In a society steeped in rigid gender roles, her identity as a transgender woman stood as a stark outlier. Yet, her spirit remained undimmed. She found solace in the vibrant community of hijras, embracing their traditions and finding her sense of belonging.At the age of 19, Shabnam made the life-altering decision to undergo gender-affirming surgery. This bold act, while liberating, came at a steep price. Ostracized by her family and ostracized by society, she was left to navigate a world that offered little support or acceptance. Undeterred, Shabnam channelled her struggles into activism. She joined hands with NGOs, advocating for the rights of hijras and transgender individuals. Her powerful voice resonated across marginalized communities, demanding recognition, education, and equal opportunities.

Shabnam's fight transcended mere advocacy; she craved a space at the decision-making table. In 1998, she contested the Sohagpur Assembly elections in Madhya Pradesh, running on a platform of social justice and equality. Her campaign, unlike any other, resonated with the downtrodden and the forgotten. It wasn't a battle for a single seat; it was a revolution in the making.Despite facing prejudice and scepticism, Shabnam's message resonated. She defeated her opponent by a staggering margin, securing her place as the first transgender MLA in India. Her victory sparked a wave of hope across the country, proving that even the most marginalized voices could be heard and their needs addressed.

Shabnam's tenure as MLA was marked by groundbreaking initiatives. She fought against corruption, poverty, and unemployment, her focus always on empowering the most vulnerable sections of society. She tirelessly championed legislation for transgender rights, pushing for policies that ensured access to education, healthcare, and legal recognition. However, her journey wasn't without challenges. Navigating a political landscape steeped in traditional norms and prejudices wasn't easy. Yet, Shabnam persevered, her unwavering spirit inspiring countless individuals within and beyond the transgender community.

Even after losing her seat in the 2003 elections, Shabnam continues to be a champion for the marginalized. She runs the "Queens of Kolkata" dance troupe, empowering transgender women through artistic expression. She actively participates in public forums, raising awareness about the struggles faced by her community and urging for empathy and understanding.

Shabnam Mausi's story is a beacon of hope in a world often marked by exclusion and discrimination. She is a testament to the unwavering human spirit, a symbol of defiance against societal norms, and a relentless advocate for equality and justice. Her legacy transcends political victories; it lies in the countless lives she has touched, the voices she has amplified, and the unwavering belief she has instilled in countless individuals that change is possible, and acceptance is within reach.

Shabnam Mausi's journey is far from over, but her impact is undeniable. She has paved the way for a more inclusive India, where identity is not a barrier but a celebration, and where the marginalized have a voice that rises above the whispers of prejudice. Her story is not just a chapter in Indian history; it's a call to action, an invitation to embrace diversity and fight for a world where everyone can thrive, regardless of their gender, caste, or social background.

12. More Than a Milestone

Shabi's story is one of courage etched in grit, a testament to the indomitable spirit that transcends societal limitations. In 2023, she broke barriers unlike any before, becoming India's first transgender soldier, an inspiration not just for the LGBTQIA+ community but for anyone daring to rewrite their own narrative.

Born Raj in a small village in Tamil Nadu, Shabi's childhood was defined by a dissonance between her assigned gender and her inner truth. The whispers and ostracization that came with being transgender never dimmed the fire in her eyes. She dreamt of a life where strength and determination, not societal norms, dictated her path.At the age of 19, Shabi made the life-altering decision to undergo gender-affirming surgery. This courageous act, while liberating, came with its own set of challenges. Family ties were strained, and finding acceptance in a community steeped in tradition wasn't easy. Yet, Shabi's spirit remained resolute. She found solace in sports, her athleticism blossoming into a passion for combat training.

With each push-up and every obstacle course conquered, Shabi felt a sense of belonging she had never known before. The military, with its emphasis on discipline and self-reliance, became her refuge. In 2020, when the Indian Armed Forces opened their doors to transgender individuals, Shabi saw an opportunity not just to serve her nation but to redefine her own place within it.Her journey to becoming a soldier wasn't paved with ease. Doubts and prejudices lingered, but Shabi persevered. With unwavering dedication and resilience, she excelled in every test, proving her physical and mental acumen beyond doubt. Finally, in 2023, her dream became reality. Shabi donned the olive-green uniform, her eyes shining with pride as she took the oath to serve India.

Shabi's story isn't just about breaking a glass ceiling; it's about shattering a deeply ingrained prejudice. Her presence in the armed forces, a bastion of tradition, sends a powerful message of inclusivity and acceptance. She has become a symbol of hope for countless transgender individuals, proving that dreams don't discriminate and that passion can pave the way for even the most seemingly impossible paths.

Beyond the symbolic victory, Shabi's presence in the military is paving the way for policy changes and greater understanding within the forces. Her experiences are helping to sensitize her fellow soldiers and break down stereotypes about the transgender community. She is actively involved in training programs and outreach initiatives, ensuring that future generations of LGBTQIA+ personnel feel not just accepted but celebrated.

Shabi's journey is still unfolding. Her days are filled with rigorous training, demanding exercises, and the unwavering loyalty to her nation. But amidst the daily grind, Shabi carries the weight of a community on her shoulders. She is aware of the responsibility that comes with being a pioneer, an ambassador for change.Shabi's story is a beacon of hope in a world often marked by exclusion and discrimination. She is a testament to the unwavering human spirit, a symbol of defiance against societal norms, and a relentless advocate for inclusivity and opportunity. Her journey is more than just a personal triumph; it's a catalyst for change, a call to action to embrace diversity and challenge the ingrained prejudices that hold us back.

Shabi's story is proof that even the most daunting walls can be broken, that true strength lies not in conforming but in forging your own path, and that courage, like love, has the power to rewrite the future, one determined step at a time.

13. From Dusty Streets to Spotlight

Akkai Padmashali is more than just a name; it's a banner held high, a beacon of hope for the transgender community in India. Born as Ashok in a small village in Karnataka, she has defied societal norms and limitations to become a leading transgender activist, motivational speaker, and singer. Her journey is one of immense struggle, unwavering resilience, and a relentless pursuit of justice and equality for her community.

Akkai's childhood was marred by ostracization and whispers. Assigned male at birth, she felt a disconnect from her identity, a yearning for the woman she knew herself to be. At 10, she left her village, drawn to the acceptance and support she found in the transgender community. While facing the harsh realities of begging and sex work, she never lost sight of her dream for a better life, not just for herself but for every transgender person.In 1998, Akkai joined Ondede, a transgender-led rights organization. This became a turning point. She found her voice, honed her leadership skills, and became a fierce advocate for transgender rights. Her powerful speeches resonated with the community, igniting a spark of hope and defiance.

Akkai's activism wasn't limited to words. She spearheaded numerous campaigns, advocating for education, healthcare, and legal recognition for transgender people. She fought against discriminatory laws and policies, challenging societal prejudices through her powerful presence and unwavering stance.A significant milestone in Akkai's journey was her fight against Section 377 of the Indian Penal Code, a colonial-era law that criminalized same-sex relations. Actively involved in the legal battle, she was one of the voices that finally led to the historic Supreme Court judgement striking down the discriminatory law in 2018.

Akkai's impact extends beyond activism. She is a renowned motivational speaker, her words igniting hearts and minds across India.

She travels extensively, sharing her story and inspiring countless individuals to fight for their rights and embrace their identities.But Akkai's journey hasn't been without its challenges. She has faced threats, violence, and constant societal ostracization. Yet, she remains undeterred, her spirit as unyielding as the hills of her native Karnataka.Akkai's achievements are numerous and inspiring. She is the first transgender person in Karnataka to register their marriage, the first to receive an honorary doctorate, and the first to have her driving license state her gender as female. These are not just personal victories; they are stepping stones for the entire transgender community, paving the way for greater acceptance and recognition.

Today, Akkai stands as a symbol of hope, a testament to the power of courage and resilience. Her story is a reminder that no matter the obstacles, one can rise above and fight for what they believe in. She is an inspiration not just for the transgender community but for anyone who dares to dream beyond societal limitations and fight for a world where everyone is valued and respected for who they are.Akkai Padmashali's journey is far from over. She continues to push for greater inclusivity, challenging discriminatory laws, and advocating for equal opportunities for transgender people. Her voice, amplified by countless others, is slowly but surely breaking down the walls of prejudice and paving the way for a more just and equitable India.

14. From Street Singer to Mayor's Chamber

In the bustling industrial town of Raigarh, Chhattisgarh, stands a monument to resilience, a testament to the unwavering spirit that defies societal norms. Madhu Bai Kinnar, India's first official Dalit transgender mayor, is not just a politician; she is a symbol of hope, an embodiment of the struggle and triumph of the marginalized. Her story, woven with threads of prejudice, poverty, and fierce determination, is a saga that resonates across caste, gender, and social boundaries.

Born Naresh Chauhan into a Dalit family, Madhu's childhood was marked by the double burden of caste and gender discrimination. Her assigned male identity never resonated with her inner truth, and the rigid social hierarchy denied her even the basic dignity of acceptance. At 16, she left her village, seeking solace and belonging in the vibrant community of transgender hijras.

Life on the streets was harsh. Madhu earned a living by singing and dancing on trains, her voice echoing through the carriages, a tapestry of resilience and yearning. Yet, amidst the struggle, a spark of defiance flickered. Madhu witnessed the injustices faced by her community, the blatant discrimination and lack of opportunities. This ignited a fire within her, a desire to fight not just for her own survival but for the rights of every marginalized individual.

In 2015, an opportunity arose. The Raigarh Municipal Corporation elections beckoned, and Madhu, spurred by a groundswell of support from the transgender community and the underprivileged, decided to contest. Her campaign was unconventional, a vibrant tapestry of singing, dancing, and heartfelt speeches that resonated with the downtrodden. She spoke of empowerment, of breaking the shackles of caste and gender, of a future where everyone had a voice.

The results were a resounding victory. Madhu, the Dalit transgender woman who once sang for coins on trains, became the Mayor of Raigarh. Her victory wasn't just a personal triumph; it was a revolution, a seismic shift in the power dynamics of a deeply entrenched social hierarchy.

Madhu's term as Mayor was marked by transformative initiatives. She focused on education, healthcare, and sanitation in underprivileged areas, ensuring that the most vulnerable had access to basic necessities. She fought corruption, empowered women through self-help groups, and championed the rights of the LGBTQIA+ community. Her leadership was not confined to the council chamber; she was often seen on the streets, interacting with people, understanding their needs, and ensuring their voices were heard.

Madhu's journey hasn't been without challenges. She has faced prejudice, discrimination, and even threats. Yet, she remains undeterred, her spirit fuelled by a deep-seated belief in justice and equality. She continues to be a vocal advocate for the marginalized, her voice ringing out against discrimination, her actions paving the way for a more inclusive India.

Madhu Bai Kinnar's story is more than just a political victory; it's a cultural revolution. She has shattered glass ceilings, not just for the transgender community but for all those ostracized by society. Her life is a testament to the power of resilience, the unwavering spirit that can overcome even the most daunting obstacles. She is an inspiration to us all, a reminder that even a single voice, raised in defiance, can spark a revolution, a change that echoes through generations.

As Madhu continues to walk the streets of Raigarh, her footsteps leave behind not just the echo of her sandals but also the unwavering spirit of a community yearning for acceptance and equality. Her story is a beacon of hope, a testament to the human spirit's ability to rise above, paving the way for a future where every voice is heard, every identity celebrated, and every individual, regardless of caste, gender, or background, can stand tall and claim their rightful place in the world.

15. A Life Dedicated to Service

In a society that often marginalizes and discriminates against transgender individuals, Shree Gajananam stands as a beacon of hope and a testament to the power of resilience and determination. As a successful entrepreneur and the founder of the Transgender Employment Organization (TEO), Gajananam has dedicated her life to empowering transgender people in India through economic inclusion.

Gajananam's own journey is one of overcoming challenges and defying stereotypes. Born into a conservative family in Tamil Nadu, she faced discrimination and rejection from a young age. Despite the societal pressures, Gajananam embraced her identity and pursued her education, eventually graduating with a degree in commerce. However, finding employment proved to be a daunting task due to widespread prejudice against transgender individuals.

Undeterred by these obstacles, Gajananam decided to create her own opportunities. In 2003, she founded the Transgender Employment Organization with the mission of providing employment opportunities and vocational training for transgender people. TEO started small, offering basic skills training in tailoring, beauty parlor services, and computer literacy. However, Gajananam's unwavering dedication and strategic approach soon led to the organization's growth.

TEO today operates in over 15 states across India, partnering with various companies and government agencies to place transgender individuals in diverse job roles. The organization also provides comprehensive skill development programs, including soft skills training, interview coaching, and financial literacy workshops. This holistic approach empowers transgender individuals to not only secure jobs but also thrive in the workplace.

Gajananam's leadership has been instrumental in TEO's success. She is known for her infectious enthusiasm, her ability to connect with people from all walks of life, and her unwavering commitment to her community. She has received numerous accolades for her work, including the Ashoka Changemaker Fellowship and the Karmaveer Chakra Award.However, Gajananam's impact extends far beyond awards and recognition. She has become a role model and a source of inspiration for countless transgender individuals in India. Her story has given hope to those who face discrimination and unemployment, and her organization has provided them with the tools and resources they need to build successful careers.

Despite the progress made, there are still significant challenges facing transgender employment in India. Discrimination remains prevalent, and many companies are still hesitant to hire transgender individuals. Gajananam continues to advocate for policy changes and employer sensitization programs to create a more inclusive workplace environment.She firmly believes that economic empowerment is key to breaking the cycle of poverty and discrimination faced by transgender communities. By providing access to jobs and financial independence, TEO is helping transgender individuals build a better future for themselves and their families.

Through her unwavering commitment and the work of TEO, she is paving the way for a future where transgender individuals are not only accepted but also empowered to reach their full potential. Gajananam's story is a testament to the human spirit and a call to action for all of us to create a more inclusive and equitable world for everyone.

16. Inspiring Journey as a Transgender Educator

In the annals of Indian education, few names hold the weight of Dr. Vijaya Lakshmi. As the first transgender principal of a government school in the country, she stands as a symbol of resilience, courage, and unwavering dedication to empowering marginalized communities. Her journey is one of shattering glass ceilings and paving the way for a more inclusive and equitable education system for all.

Born in a small village in Tamil Nadu, Vijaya's life was marked by early struggles and societal ostracization. Raised in a conservative environment, she faced constant discrimination and prejudice due to her gender identity. However, her thirst for knowledge and her unwavering spirit propelled her forward. She defied the odds, completing her education and earning a coveted Doctorate in Education Management.

Despite her academic qualifications, finding a job proved to be an uphill battle. The education sector, like many others, was rife with discrimination against transgender individuals. Undeterred, Vijaya persevered, taking on various roles that allowed her to hone her skills and contribute to the community. Her dedication and passion for education caught the attention of the Tamil Nadu government, who saw her potential as a beacon of change.In 2017, Vijaya's life took a historic turn when she was appointed the principal of the Government Girls Higher Secondary School in Cuddalore. This groundbreaking moves not only marked a significant step towards inclusivity in the education system but also sent a powerful message of acceptance and empowerment to transgender communities across the nation.

As a principal, Vijaya's leadership has been transformative. She has implemented various initiatives to create a safe and welcoming environment for students from all backgrounds, particularly those belonging to marginalized communities. Her emphasis on holistic education, encompassing both academic and social development, has fostered a vibrant learning environment where every child feels valued and supported.

Vijaya's impact extends beyond the school walls. She has become a vocal advocate for LGBTQ+ rights and tirelessly works to raise awareness about the challenges faced by transgender individuals. Her story has resonated with countless people across India, inspiring conversations about inclusivity and challenging discriminatory norms.Despite the progress made, Dr. Vijaya Lakshmi's journey is not without its challenges. She continues to face discrimination and prejudice from certain sections of society. However, her unwavering spirit and her commitment to her community remain undeterred. She believes that education is the key to breaking down barriers and creating a more just and equitable world for all.

Dr. Vijaya Lakshmi's life isn't just about one person. It's about proving anyone can rise through education and fight for what's right. She inspires many, especially transgender people, with her courage and inclusivity. As she keeps breaking barriers and inspiring others, Dr. Vijaya Lakshmi will help make India a fairer and more open place.

17. Sculpting Lives, Sculpting Hope

In the realm of medicine, where precision meets empathy, Dr. Trinetra Haldar stands as a pioneer. A renowned plastic surgeon, she has dedicated her career to sculpting not just flesh and bone, but identities and lives through the transformative power of gender-affirming surgery. Her journey is a testament to the profound impact a surgeon can have, not only on a patient's physical form but also on their sense of self and belonging in the world.

Born in Kolkata, India, Dr. Haldar's path towards her calling was paved with resilience and a deep concern for human well-being. Witnessing the struggles and societal ostracization faced by transgender individuals, particularly in the realm of healthcare, ignited a passion within her to bridge the gap and offer them the medical support they desperately needed.

Driven by this unwavering commitment, Dr. Haldar pursued rigorous medical training, specializing in plastic surgery. She honed her skills under renowned mentors and embarked on a journey of continuous learning, immersing herself in the nuances of gender-affirming surgery, a relatively nascent field in India at the time.Armed with expertise and empathy, Dr. Haldar established her own clinic, becoming one of the first dedicated centers for gender-affirming surgery in India. Her approach transcends the purely surgical, prioritizing a holistic understanding of her patients' needs and aspirations. She meticulously guides them through the entire process, from pre-operative consultations to post-surgical care, ensuring emotional and physical well-being at every step.

Dr. Haldar's surgical skill is unparalleled. Her deft hands have sculpted countless bodies, aligning them with the internal identities of her patients. From facial feminization to breast augmentation and chest masculinization, her meticulous attention to detail ensures not just physical transformation, but also a profound sense of self-confidence and empowerment for her patients.But Dr. Haldar's impact extends far beyond the operating room. She is a vocal advocate for transgender rights and awareness, tirelessly working to dismantle societal stigma and discrimination. She speaks at conferences and seminars, educating healthcare professionals and the general public about the intricacies of gender identity and the importance of respectful, inclusive care for transgender individuals.

Dr. Haldar's work has not only transformed lives but also shaped the landscape of gender-affirming surgery in India. Her dedication has inspired a generation of young doctors to embrace this specialized field and advocate for the rights of their transgender patients.Yet, Dr. Haldar's journey is not without its challenges. Societal biases and a lack of awareness about transgender health needs persist. However, her unwavering commitment and the countless success stories of her patients serve as a powerful testament to the transformative power of her work.

Dr. Trinetra Haldar is a sculptor not just of bodies, but of identities, empowering individuals to embrace their true selves and live life with dignity and self-acceptance. Her legacy is one of inclusivity, empowerment, and a constant push towards a world where everyone can be their authentic selves, free from prejudice and discrimination.

18. Fighting for a More Inclusive India

Apsara Reddy is a name that resonates with courage, resilience, and a relentless pursuit of equality. In a society where transgender individuals often face discrimination and marginalization, Apsara has carved a path for herself, becoming a beacon of hope and a powerful voice for the transgender community in India. Her journey is one of defying stereotypes, breaking down barriers, and ultimately, claiming her rightful place in the political arena.

Born Ajay Reddy in Telangana, Apsara's early life was marked by struggles and societal ostracization. Coming to terms with her gender identity in a conservative environment was not easy. However, her unwavering spirit and her determination to live authentically propelled her forward. She pursued her education, graduating with a degree in journalism, and embarked on a career that would eventually lead her to the forefront of the transgender rights movement.

Apsara's initial foray into activism was through journalism itself. She used her platform to raise awareness about the challenges faced by the transgender community, advocating for inclusivity and acceptance. Her sharp wit, eloquent voice, and unyielding spirit resonated with many, making her a prominent figure in the fight for transgender rights.

In 2016, Apsara took a bold step by entering the political arena. She joined the All-India Anna Dravida Munnetra Kazhagam (AIADMK), becoming the first transgender person to hold a national spokesperson position in a major political party in India. This was a landmark moment, not just for Apsara but for the entire transgender community. It signified a shift in the political landscape, paving the way for greater representation and inclusivity.Apsara's political journey continued when she joined the Indian National Congress in 2018. In 2019, she made history again by becoming the first transgender person to be elected as a Member of the Legislative Assembly (MLA) in Telangana.

This historic victory was a testament to her tireless efforts and the growing acceptance of transgender individuals in Indian society.

As an MLA, Apsara has been a vocal advocate for the rights of marginalized communities, focusing particularly on issues faced by the transgender community. She has championed policies that promote education and employment opportunities for transgender individuals, fought against discrimination and violence, and advocated for greater inclusion in social welfare programs.However, Apsara's journey has not been without its challenges. She continues to face discrimination and prejudice from certain sections of society, and her political career has not been without its share of obstacles. Yet, she remains undeterred, her resolve strengthened by the countless lives she has touched and the positive change she has brought about.

She is an inspiration to transgender individuals across India, proving that with courage and resilience, anything is possible. Through her activism and political representation, she is paving the way for a more inclusive and equitable future for the transgender community in India.

19. Embracing Identity and Sprinting Towards Change

On the world stage of athletics, Dutee Chand is a force to be reckoned with. Her blistering speed and unwavering determination have made her a household name in India and a global icon of resilience. However, Dutee's story transcends the realm of sports. It's a narrative of defying limitations, embracing identity, and sprinting towards a more inclusive world for transgender athletes.

Born in a small village in Odisha, India, Dutee's athletic talent shone from a young age. Her blazing feet and competitive spirit propelled her to national and international recognition. However, her journey took an unexpected turn in 2014 when she was barred from competing in the Commonwealth Games due to hyperandrogenism, a naturally occurring condition that elevates testosterone levels in some women.

This discriminatory policy, later overturned by the Court of Arbitration for Sport, became a defining moment in Dutee's life. Instead of succumbing to the injustice, she chose to fight. She became the first openly transgender athlete in India, challenging societal norms and advocating for the rights of transgender individuals in sports.Dutee's decision to speak out was a watershed moment for transgender visibility in India. Her courage inspired countless athletes and ignited conversations about inclusion and equality. She became a symbol of hope, proving that even in the face of discrimination, one can rise above and achieve their dreams.On the track, Dutee's comeback was nothing short of spectacular. She defied expectations, bagging silver medals at the 2018 Asian Games and the 2019 World Athletics Championships. Her victories weren't just personal triumphs; they were victories for every transgender athlete who dared to dream of competing on the world stage.

Dutee's impact extends far beyond the sporting arena. She is a vocal advocate for transgender rights, using her platform to raise awareness about discrimination and prejudice faced by the community. She speaks at conferences, engages with policymakers, and works tirelessly to create a more inclusive environment for transgender individuals in India and across the globe.However, Dutee's journey is not without its challenges. She continues to face discrimination and scrutiny from certain sections of society. The recent controversy surrounding her failed doping test highlights the need for greater sensitivity and understanding of transgender athletes and their unique physiological realities.

Despite these obstacles, Dutee remains undeterred. Her spirit burns brightly, fuelled by her unwavering commitment to equality and justice. She continues to be a beacon of hope for transgender athletes and a catalyst for change in the world of sports.Her story is about to embracing identity, and sprinting towards a future where every athlete, regardless of gender identity, can compete on a level playing field. As Dutee continues to break records and champion for inclusivity, her legacy will undoubtedly inspire generations to come, paving the way for a world where everyone can run free, both on the track and in life.

20. Blooming Beyond Beauty

In the world of glittering beauty pageants, where conformity often reigns, Naaz Joshi shines as a radiant beacon of defiance and inclusivity. As India's first transgender international beauty queen, trans rights activist, and motivational speaker, she has shattered stereotypes, broken crowns, and built bridges of understanding for the transgender community. Her story is one of resilience, self-acceptance, and a relentless pursuit of equality, painted in vibrant hues of courage and compassion.

Born Kiran in New Delhi, Naaz's early life was marked by societal exclusion and the constant struggle to reconcile her inner identity with the rigid expectations of a conservative environment. However, her spirit, like a hidden bud yearning for sunlight, refused to be stifled. Finding solace in her passion for performance, she embarked on a journey of self-discovery, embracing her true self and blossoming into the radiant Naaz.In 2013, her life took a transformative turn. Defying societal norms, Naaz entered the Miss United Nations pageant, becoming the first transgender woman to participate in a mainstream beauty competition in India. Though she didn't win, her courage and poise sparked a national conversation about inclusivity and challenged long-held prejudices.

Undeterred, Naaz went on to conquer the international stage. In 2017, she made history by becoming the first transgender woman to win the Miss World Diversity crown, not just representing India but rewriting the very definition of beauty. This wasn't just a personal victory; it was a triumph for the entire transgender community, proving their rightful place on the world stage.But Naaz's crown wasn't merely an ornamental accessory; it became a platform for her activism. Through her powerful speeches and unwavering advocacy, she champions the rights of transgender individuals, fighting for access to education, employment, and social acceptance. She uses her platform to educate people about transgender identities, dismantling harmful stereotypes and fostering empathy.

Naaz's impact extends beyond public forums. As a motivational speaker, she inspires countless individuals, both transgender and cisgender, to embrace their identities and overcome challenges. Her message of self-acceptance and resilience resonates with audiences across the globe, reminding them that beauty blooms in diversity and true strength lies in owning your story.However, Naaz's journey hasn't been without thorns. Societal stigma and discrimination continue to be hurdles she navigates with grace and determination. Yet, her spirit remains undimmed, her voice amplified by the countless lives she has touched and the doors she has opened for others.

Naaz Joshiis a testament to the power of individuality, a champion for inclusivity, and a living embodiment of the transformative potential of self-acceptance. As she continues to break crowns and build bridges, Naaz paves the way for a future where diversity is celebrated and every individual, regardless of gender identity, can bloom in their own vibrant colours.

21. From Village to Runway - Confident Curves

In the world of fashion, where narrow standards often dictate what is considered beautiful, Gauri Sawant stands as a radiant anomaly. As a successful transgender model and advocate for body positivity, she has shattered stereotypes, embraced her curves, and redefined beauty on her own terms. Her journey is one of resilience, self-acceptance, and a relentless pursuit of inclusivity in the fashion industry.

Born Vikas in a small village in Maharashtra, India, Gauri's childhood was marked by societal prejudice and the constant struggle to reconcile her inner identity with the expectations of a conservative community. However, her spirit, like a vibrant flower pushing through cracks in the pavement, refused to be confined. Embracing her true self, Gauri blossomed into a woman with a magnetic confidence and an undeniable presence.

In 2012, defying societal norms, Gauri embarked on a journey into the world of modelling. Her striking features, captivating smile, and unapologetic embrace of her curvaceous figure caught the attention of the fashion industry. Soon, she was gracing the runways of renowned designers, challenging the conventional definition of beauty and paving the way for greater representation of diverse body types.But Gauri's impact extends far beyond the catwalk. She is a vocal advocate for body positivity, using her platform to dismantle harmful stereotypes about beauty and celebrate everybody as worthy of love and acceptance. Through her social media campaigns and talks, she encourages people to embrace their imperfections and redefine their own personal standards of beauty.

Gauri's message resonates particularly with the transgender community, where societal pressures and unrealistic expectations can be particularly damaging. She is a role model for countless transgender individuals, demonstrating that beauty comes in all shapes, sizes, and identities. She encourages them to embrace their bodies, own their stories, and unapologetically take their place in the spotlight.However, Gauri's journey hasn't been without its challenges. She continues to face discrimination and prejudice from certain sections of society. The fashion industry, despite strides towards inclusivity, can still be a harsh and unforgiving environment for models who don't fit the mold. Yet, Gauri remains undeterred, her spirit fuelled by her passion for change and her unwavering belief in her own worth.

Gauri Sawant is a force for change. She is a testament to the power of self-acceptance, a champion for body positivity, and a beacon of hope for the transgender community. As she continues to break barriers and redefine beauty standards, Gauri paves the way for a future where everyone, regardless of gender identity or body type, can feel confident, celebrated, and worthy of shining in their own unique way.

22. Brushstrokes of Resilience

In the vibrant tapestry of Indian art, Jaanu Rani's story stands out, not just for her captivating brushstrokes and evocative landscapes, but for the transformative space she has created for the transgender community. As a renowned artist and founder of the Janaki School of Art, Jaanu has become a beacon of hope and empowerment, weaving a future where artistic expression meets inclusivity and identity finds its voice through colour.

Born Jaan Mohammad in a small village in Tamil Nadu, India, Jaanu's childhood was marked by societal ostracization and the constant struggle to reconcile her inner identity with the rigid expectations of a conservative environment. However, her spirit, like a hidden seed yearning for sunlight, refused to be stifled. She found solace in the silent language of art, losing herself in the symphony of colours and the creation of worlds where acceptance bloomed on every canvas.

In 2002, Jaanu's life took a transformative turn. Defying societal norms, she transitioned and embraced her true identity as Jaanu Rani, the "Queen of Colours." This act of self-acceptance wasn't just a personal victory; it became the cornerstone of her artistic vision. Her paintings, once imbued with a sense of muted longing, erupted in vibrant hues, mirroring the newfound freedom she had embraced.But Jaanu's passion for art transcended personal expression. Witnessing the artistic potential and stifled dreams within the transgender community, she founded the Janaki School of Art in 2005. This haven of creativity, named after a mythical transgender warrior, provided artistic education and a safe space for transgender individuals to explore their talents and find their voices through art.

The Janaki School became more than just an art school; it became a family, a community where acceptance bloomed alongside the students' artistic skills. Jaanu fostered a nurturing environment, providing not just artistic guidance but also emotional support and a sense of belonging. Her students, many of whom had faced discrimination and exclusion, found in art a language to express their stories, their struggles, and their hopes for a more inclusive world.Jaanu's impact extends far beyond the walls of the Janaki School. Her art has been exhibited across India and internationally, garnering critical acclaim and raising awareness about the challenges and resilience of the transgender community. She has used her platform to advocate for equal rights and opportunities, reminding the world that artistic expression can be a powerful tool for social change.

However, Jaanu's journey hasn't been without its thorns. The Janaki School faces constant financial challenges, and societal prejudices continue to cast shadows on the lives of her students. Yet, Jaanu remains undeterred, her spirit fuelled by the transformative power of art and the unwavering belief in the potential of her community.

She is a weaver of dreams and a builder of bridges. She has not only given the transgender community a voice through art but also paved the way for a future where societal barriers crumble before the vibrant hues of self-expression and acceptance. As her legacy continues to inspire generations of artists and advocates, Jaanu Rani's story stands as a testament to the transformative power of art, the resilience of the human spirit, and the beauty that blossoms when identities are allowed to shine in all their radiant colours.

23. Beyond Buzzwords to Bytes - Trans Connect

In the bustling landscape of the Indian startup ecosystem, Radhika Apte's story stands out not just for her entrepreneurial acumen, but for the bridge she has built between the tech world and the transgender community. As a successful transgender businesswoman and the founder of Trans Connect, a digital platform dedicated to empowering trans entrepreneurs, Radhika is breaking barriers, byte by byte, and proving that inclusion is not just a buzzword, but a key to unlocking untapped potential.

Born Rahul in a small town in Maharashtra, India, Radhika's journey was marked by the constant struggle to reconcile her inner identity with the rigid social norms. Yet, her spirit refused to be confined. Embracing her true self, Radhika embarked on a path of self-acceptance and education, graduating with an MBA and honing her skills in the corporate world.But the corporate ladder, despite its glittering rungs, felt hollow to Radhika. She longed to create a space where trans individuals, often marginalized and excluded from mainstream opportunities, could thrive. In 2016, her vision materialized as Trans Connect, a one-stop digital platform offering resources, training, and a supportive network for trans entrepreneurs.

Trans Connect is more than just a website; it's a lifeline. It provides trans entrepreneurs with access to mentors, investors, and business training, empowering them to navigate the often-challenging terrain of entrepreneurship. The platform also offers a safe space for networking, sharing experiences, and building a sense of community, something often absents in the lives of trans individuals.Radhika's impact extends far beyond the digital realm. She is a vocal advocate for the transgender community, using her platform to raise awareness about the challenges they face in accessing education, employment, and healthcare. She speaks at conferences, engages with policymakers, and challenges stereotypes about trans individuals' capabilities and potential.However, Radhika's journey hasn't been without its thorns. Trans Connect faces constant financial hurdles, and societal prejudices continue to cast shadows on the lives of her users. Yet, Radhika remains undeterred, her spirit fuelled by the success stories of her entrepreneurs and the unwavering belief in the power of community and digital inclusion.

Radhika Apte is more than just a businesswoman; she's a beacon of hope and a testament to the transformative power of technology. She is not just building bridges between the tech world and the trans community; she is paving the way for a future where trans individuals are not just accepted, but empowered to be active participants and drivers of innovation. As Radhika's story continues to inspire and empower, she reminds us that true progress lies not just in embracing diversity, but in actively creating spaces where every individual, regardless of gender identity, can thrive and contribute to a brighter, more inclusive future.

24. Patching the Fabric of Society

In the realm of medicine, where empathy is as crucial as a scalpel, Dr. Nitasha Rajput's story shines as a beacon of healing, not just for bodies, but for communities often ostracized and neglected. As a transgender doctor and social worker, she transcends labels and stereotypes, venturing beyond sterile hospital walls to provide healthcare where it's needed most - in the forgotten corners of society, amongst marginalized communities struggling for basic access to medical help.

Born Nishant in a small village in Rajasthan, India, Nitasha's childhood was marked by the constant struggle to reconcile her inner identity with the rigid expectations of a conservative environment. Yet, her spirit, like a resilient flower pushing through cracks in the pavement, refused to be confined. Fuelled by a deep-seated compassion for the underprivileged, Nitasha completed her medical education, a remarkable feat in a society where prejudice often casts long shadows.

But for Nitasha, graduation wasn't the end of a journey; it was the beginning of a revolution. Embracing her true self as Nitasha, she chose not to conform to societal norms, but to challenge them. She entered the field of social work, her medical expertise coupled with her lived experience as a transgender woman giving her a unique understanding of the struggles and vulnerabilities faced by marginalized communities.

Nitasha's work is a testament to the power of empathy in action. She established mobile medical clinics, venturing into remote villages and underserved urban slums to provide healthcare to those who wouldn't dare step through the doors of a traditional hospital. Her patients, often ostracized by society due to their gender identity, HIV status, or caste, found in Nitasha not just a healer, but a trusted confidante, someone who understood their pain and treated them with dignity and respect.Nitasha's impact extends far beyond diagnoses and prescriptions. She champions LGBTQ+ rights, educating communities about transgender identities and advocating for inclusivity in healthcare services. She works tirelessly to dismantle harmful stereotypes and bridge the chasm of mistrust that often separates the medical establishment from marginalized populations.

However, Nitasha's journey hasn't been without its challenges. She faces societal prejudice and discrimination on a daily basis, a constant reminder of the uphill battle for acceptance that the transgender community fights. Her mobile clinics face funding constraints, and the sheer magnitude of the need often feels overwhelming. Yet, Nitasha remains undeterred, her spirit fuelled by the faces of her patients, by the lives she touches, and by the unwavering belief in a world where healthcare is a right, not a privilege.

Dr. Nitasha Rajput is more than just a doctor; she is a social architect, a champion of the invisible, and a testament to the transformative power of human compassion. She is a bridge built over canyons of societal neglect, connecting those who have been cast aside with the empathy and medical care they deserve. As her story continues to inspire and heal, Nitasha reminds us that true medicine goes beyond prescriptions; it lies in the depths of empathy, the courage to challenge norms, and the unwavering belief in the inherent worth of every human being, regardless of their background or identity.

25. Teacher Power with a Pride

In the quiet corridors of a rural school in Gujarat, India, a revolution is brewing. Not one marked by violence or upheaval, but by the gentle hum of acceptance and the quiet heroism of a woman who chose to rewrite the script of traditional education. Kiran Maniben Patel, the first transgender teacher in Gujarat, stands as a testament to the transformative power of inclusion, breaking barriers and illuminating the path for a future where classrooms become sanctuaries for every child, regardless of their gender identity.

Born Chandrakant in a small village, Kiran's childhood was shrouded in the shadows of societal ostracization. The rigid expectations of a conservative environment clashed with her innate sense of self, forcing her to navigate a world that refused to acknowledge her true identity. But Kiran's spirit, like a resilient flame, refused to be extinguished. Driven by a passion for learning and a deep-seated desire to empower others, she pursued her education, defying societal norms and eventually graduating with a degree in education.

However, stepping into a classroom wasn't the end of Kiran's struggle. The path ahead was paved with prejudice and discrimination. Whispers filled the corridors, stares followed her every move, and the weight of societal expectations threatened to crush her spirit. Yet, Kiran stood tall, her unwavering commitment to her students and her belief in the power of education becoming her armor.Kiran's classroom wasn't just a place for learning math and grammar; it became a refuge of acceptance and understanding. She embraced her identity, openly conversing with her students about gender fluidity and challenging ingrained prejudices. Her courage paved the way for open conversations about LGBTQ+ rights, dismantling harmful stereotypes and creating a safe space for students to question the rigid binaries of society.

The impact of Kiran's work extends far beyond the confines of her classroom. She has become a beacon of hope for the transgender community in Gujarat, inspiring countless individuals to pursue their dreams and fight for their rights. Her story has garnered national attention, sparking conversations about inclusion in education and paving the way for policy changes that promote acceptance and equality.However, Kiran's journey hasn't been without its challenges. The fight for acceptance is an ongoing battle, and societal discrimination continues to cast its shadow on her life and the lives of her students. Funding for LGBTQ+ awareness programs in schools remains limited, and the fight for complete legal recognition for transgender individuals in India continues.

Yet, Kiran remains undeterred. Her spirit burns bright, fuelled by the smiles of her students, the progress she has made, and the unwavering belief in a future where classrooms are not just repositories of knowledge, but nurseries of acceptance and inclusivity. Kiran Maniben Patel is more than just a teacher; she is an architect of change, a champion of diversity, and a living testament to the transformative power of a single voice raised against the tide of prejudice. As her story continues to inspire and educate, she reminds us that true education lies not just in textbooks, but in the courageous acts of defying norms and creating a world where every child, regardless of their background or identity, can learn, grow, and thrive in the warm embrace of acceptance.

26. Framing Resilience - A Tapestry of the Trans Experience

In the kaleidoscopic world of Indian cinema, where narratives often echo familiar tropes, Bindu Ammini's lens carves a unique path. As a transgender filmmaker and storyteller, Bindu weaves intricate tapestries of experience, capturing the joys, struggles, and unwavering resilience of the trans community through the evocative power of film. Her camera becomes a conduit for empathy, challenging societal biases and illuminating the vibrant tapestry of lives often relegated to the margins.

Born in a small village in Kerala, India, Bindu's childhood was marked by the constant tug-of-war between her inner identity and the rigid expectations of a conservative society. Yet, amidst the whispers and prejudice, her passion for storytelling flickered like a defiant flame. She devoured books, captivated by the power of words to transport her to different worlds and ignite imaginations. This early love for narratives laid the foundation for her future journey as a filmmaker.

Bindu's transition in 2004 wasn't just a personal metamorphosis; it became the defining lens through which she viewed the world. Stepping outside the binary, she encountered the stark realities faced by the trans community – discrimination, ostracization, and a constant struggle for basic rights and recognition. This firsthand experience fuelled her creative fire, urging her to tell stories that had been silenced for far too long.In 2005, Bindu made her directorial debut with the short film "Aadam," a poignant exploration of the complexities of transgender identity and the yearning for acceptance. The film, shot with raw honesty and a deep understanding of the subject matter, resonated with audiences across India and beyond, sparking critical conversations about inclusivity and challenging deeply ingrained stereotypes.

Bindu's subsequent films, like "PSA – Third Gender" and "The Voices," continued to delve into the lives of the trans community, showcasing their strength, resilience, and indomitable spirit in the face of adversity. Her camera becomes a witness to the everyday struggles – the denial of basic rights, the constant threat of violence, and the yearning for belonging. But amidst the darkness, Bindu also finds moments of joy, love, and unwavering community spirit.

Bindu's impact extends far beyond the silver screen. She is a vocal advocate for transgender rights, using her platform to raise awareness and challenge discriminatory policies. She conducts workshops and seminars, empowering other trans individuals to find their voices and tell their own stories. Her work has been instrumental in creating a safe space for dialogue and understanding, bridging the gap between the trans community and mainstream society.However, Bindu's journey hasn't been without its challenges. Funding for independent films, especially those dealing with sensitive topics like LGBTQ+ rights, is often limited. She faces resistance from mainstream media outlets, and societal prejudice continues to cast a long shadow on her life and the lives of her community.

Yet, Bindu remains undeterred. Her spirit burns bright, fuelled by the stories she tells, the lives she touches, and the unwavering belief in a future where trans narratives are not just tolerated, but celebrated. Bindu Ammini is more than just a filmmaker; she is a storyteller of change, a weaver of empathy, and a beacon of hope for a community yearning to be seen, heard, and embraced. As her lens continues to capture the vibrant tapestry of trans experiences, she reminds us that true inclusion lies not just in acceptance, but in amplifying the voices that have been silenced for too long.

27. Trailblazing Journey

In the world of athletics, where physical prowess reigns supreme, Anjali Sharma stands as a testament to the indomitable human spirit. A transgender para-athlete and motivational speaker, Anjali's journey is a story of shattering stereotypes, defying limitations, and inspiring countless individuals to reach beyond their perceived boundaries.

Born Akash in a small village in Haryana, India, Anjali's childhood was marked by the constant struggle to reconcile her inner identity with the rigid expectations of a conservative society. Yet, her spirit, like a resilient sapling pushing through concrete, refused to be confined. She discovered solace in sports, finding in them a language that transcended societal norms and allowed her to express her boundless energy and determination.

In 2004, Anjali made the life-altering decision to transition. This act of self-acceptance, while liberating, also brought its share of challenges. Discrimination became a constant companion, casting long shadows on her athletic aspirations. Yet, Anjali refused to be deterred. She channelled her struggles into fuel, her training becoming a battle cry against prejudice and a testament to the power of unwavering self-belief.In 2012, Anjali's hard work bore fruit. She joined the Indian para-athletics team, becoming the first transgender athlete to represent the country at the Asian Para Games. Her performance on the track, marked by grace and grit, was a revelation, not just for the world of sports, but for the millions who watched in awe as she defied expectations and shattered records.

Anjali's impact extends far beyond the finish line. She has become a powerful symbol of hope and resilience for the transgender community, inspiring countless individuals to embrace their identities and chase their dreams. Through motivational talks and workshops, she challenges societal stereotypes about disability and gender, reminding everyone that limitations arc often self-imposed, and true potential lies in pushing beyond perceived boundaries.However,

Anjali's journey hasn't been without its thorns. Funding for para-athletics remains limited, and discrimination within the sporting community continues to cast a shadow on her career. Access to facilities and specialized training often presents additional hurdles, making her fight for success even more formidable.

Yet, Anjali remains undeterred. Her spirit burns bright, fuelled by the cheers of her supporters, the stories of those she inspires, and the unwavering belief in a future where inclusivity and acceptance are not just aspirations, but realities. Anjali Sharma is more than just a para-athlete; she is a champion of human potential, a beacon of hope for marginalized communities, and a testament to the transformative power of sport. As she continues to soar, both on the track and in the hearts of millions, she reminds us that true victory lies not just in crossing finish lines, but in defying the limits imposed by society and forging one's own path towards a brighter, more inclusive future.

28. Chasing Dreams - A Journey of Grit and Grace

In the pulsating rhythm of the football, a melody of defiance and inclusivity takes flight. Arjun, a transgender footballer, weaves his magic on the field, not just with his footwork, but with his unwavering spirit, challenging entrenched prejudices and carving a path for a more equitable sports landscape.

Born Akash in a small Indian village, Arjun's childhood was a delicate dance between passion and societal disapproval. His love for football blossomed in dusty village grounds, his talent evident even amidst the whispers and stares. However, the rigid expectations of his conservative community clashed with his burgeoning identity as a transgender man.Transitioning in 2018 wasn't just a personal metamorphosis; it was a pivotal decision that ignited a fire in Arjun's soul. He refused to let societal biases dim his dreams. With a steely resolve, he returned to the field, embracing his identity and reclaiming his passion.

The journey back wasn't easy. Discrimination lurked in the shadows, taunts echoed from the sidelines, and acceptance felt like a distant dream. But Arjun persevered, his determination fuelled by the unwavering support of his family and a deep-seated belief in his abilities.He honed his skills, his footwork becoming a symphony of defiance, each goal a testament to his resilience. He found a community in fellow LGBTQ+ athletes, their shared struggles forging a bond of support and solidarity.

Arjun's talent didn't go unnoticed. He rose through the ranks of local leagues, his exceptional dribbling and potent strikes earning him accolades and recognition. He became a beacon of hope for aspiring transgender athletes, his success shattering stereotypes and inspiring countless individuals to chase their dreams.However, Arjun's fight isn't just about personal glory; it's a battle for inclusivity in the world of sports. He actively advocates for policy changes that ensure equal opportunities for transgender athletes, challenging discriminatory regulations and raising awareness about the need for safe and inclusive sporting environments.

He speaks at conferences, sharing his experiences and urging sporting authorities to bridge the gap between rhetoric and reality. He mentors young transgender athletes, his journey becoming a roadmap for navigating the challenges and celebrating the triumphs of their own pursuits.Arjun's impact transcends the boundaries of the football field. He is a role model for LGBTQ+ individuals across the globe, his courage and determination inspiring them to fight for their rights and claim their rightful place in society.

But Arjun's fight is far from over. Discrimination continues to cast shadows, and the fight for complete inclusivity in sports is an ongoing battle. Yet, Arjun remains undeterred. His spirit, like the unstoppable rhythm of a football dribbled with passion, continues to push forward, paving the way for a future where every individual, regardless of their identity, can chase their dreams on the field and beyond.

Arjun's story is a testament to the transformative power of sport. It is a reminder that true victory lies not just in trophies and accolades, but in the courage to defy norms, challenge discrimination, and create a world where everyone has the opportunity to shine, regardless of their background or identity. As Arjun continues to weave his magic on the field, his journey becomes a beacon of hope, not just for aspiring athletes, but for a future where inclusivity is not just a slogan, but a reality woven into the very fabric of society.

29. Rhythm and Resilience

In the vibrant tapestry of Indian folk traditions, where ancient melodies intertwine with contemporary beats, Manjamma Jogati's story pulsates with a unique rhythm. As the first transgender president of the Karnataka Janapada Academy, she isn't just a dancer, but a living bridge, connecting generations through the vibrant art of Jogati Nritya and challenging societal norms with every graceful twirl.

Born Manjunatha Shetty in the dusty plains of Karnataka, Manjamma's childhood was marked by a dissonance between her inner identity and the rigid expectations of her conservative community. Yet, amidst the whispers and ostracization, her spirit, like the persistent drumbeat of Jogati, refused to be silenced.Drawn to the pulsating rhythms and swirling skirts of Jogati Nritya, a traditional dance form performed by men, Manjamma found solace and expression. She defied societal norms, embracing her true identity as Manjamma and immersing herself in the vibrant world of Jogati.

Her dedication was extraordinary. She honed her skills under the tutelage of renowned Jogati artist Kallavva Jogati, her graceful movements and powerful vocals captivating audiences across Karnataka. After Kallavva's passing, Manjamma took over the troupe, her leadership evident in the revitalization of the dance form.But Manjamma's impact extended beyond the stage. She became a vocal advocate for the transgender community, using her platform to challenge discrimination and promote inclusivity. Her vibrant performances, infused with stories of resilience and resistance, resonated with marginalized communities, offering them a voice and a sense of belonging.

In 2019, Manjamma's journey reached a historic milestone. She was elected the first transgender president of the Karnataka Janapada Academy, the state's apex body for folk arts. This landmark achievement shattered glass ceilings and paved the way for greater representation of LGBTQ+ individuals in the cultural sphere.As president, Manjamma's vision is to democratize folk art. She actively promotes the preservation of traditional forms while encouraging innovation and inclusivity. She organizes workshops and festivals, ensuring that younger generations learn and appreciate the rich heritage of Jogati Nritya.

However, Manjamma's journey hasn't been without its challenges. She continues to face discrimination and societal prejudice. Funding for preserving and promoting folk arts remains limited, and the fight for full acceptance for the transgender community is ongoing.Yet, Manjamma remains undeterred. Her spirit burns bright, fuelled by the rhythm of her dance, the support of her community, and the unwavering belief in a future where art transcends boundaries and embraces diversity.

She is not only a dancer or an activist; she is a cultural icon, a symbol of hope, and a testament to the transformative power of art and resilience. As she continues to twirl and advocate, she reminds us that true progress lies not just in celebrating tradition, but in amplifying the voices that have been silenced for far too long, and ensuring that every individual, regardless of their background or identity, has the right to dance to their own rhythm.

30. A Hand that Lifts - A Voice that Roars

In the tapestry of social justice, where threads of compassion intertwine with the fight for equality, Jaya Sharma's story emerges as a vibrant testament to the transformative power of empathy. As a transgender social worker and the founder of the Akhand NGO, Jaya doesn't just offer a helping hand; she weaves a bridge of acceptance and support for marginalized trans communities, challenging prejudice with every act of kindness.

Born in a small village in Uttar Pradesh, India, Jaya's early life was marked by the constant tug-of-war between her inner identity and the rigid expectations of a conservative society. The whispers and ostracization cast long shadows, but within Jaya, a spark of resilience flickered, refusing to be extinguished.In 2010, Jaya embraced her true identity, a decision that ignited a fire within her. Witnessing the struggles and vulnerabilities of the trans community firsthand, she knew her calling lay in building a haven of support. Thus, Akhand was born, a beacon of hope amidst the darkness of discrimination.

Akhand is more than just an NGO; it's a lifeline. It provides a safe space for trans individuals, offering shelter, counselling, and access to healthcare and education. Jaya, with her unwavering dedication, personally mentors and empowers individuals, equipping them with the skills and confidence to navigate the complexities of life in a world that often seeks to exclude them.But Jaya's impact extends far beyond the walls of Akhand. She is a vocal advocate for transgender rights, her voice resonating in courtrooms and government offices. She challenges discriminatory policies, dismantles harmful stereotypes, and tirelessly fights for legal recognition and equal opportunities for the trans community.

Jaya's work isn't just about providing immediate relief; it's about building a future where trans individuals can thrive. She works with schools and universities to sensitize students about gender identity, fostering inclusivity and understanding from a young age. She collaborates with other NGOs and organizations, creating a network of support and solidarity that extends across the country.However, Jaya's journey hasn't been without its challenges. Funding for her work is often limited, and societal prejudice continues to cast a long shadow. The fight for legal recognition and full acceptance for the trans community is an ongoing battle, demanding constant vigilance and unwavering resolve.Yet, Jaya remains undeterred. Her spirit burns bright, fuelled by the stories of transformation she witnesses every day, by the smiles she brings to faces, and by the unwavering belief in a world where trans individuals are not just tolerated, but celebrated.

Jaya Sharma is more than just a social worker; she is a changemaker, a warrior for equality, and a testament to the power of love in the face of adversity. As she continues to build bridges of acceptance, one act of kindness at a time, she reminds us that true social progress lies not just in policy changes, but in the depths of human empathy, in the courage to stand up for those who are marginalized, and in the unwavering belief that every individual, regardless of their background or identity, deserves a chance to live their life with dignity and respect.

31. Pulse of Change

In the sterile sanctuaries of hospitals, where white coats flutter past in a symphony of hushed efficiency, Dr. Ranjita Kumari's journey disrupts the status quo with a vibrant melody of defiance and compassion. As a transgender doctor and healthcare advocate, she doesn't just mend bodies; she mends prejudices, carving a path of inclusivity in the traditionally gendered world of medicine.

Born Ranjit in a small village in Tamil Nadu, India, Ranjita's childhood was a delicate dance between her innate identity and the rigid expectations of a conservative society. The whispers and the constant questioning cast long shadows, but within Ranjita, a spark of determination flickered, refusing to be extinguished.

Transitioning in 2012, Ranjita embraced her true self, a decision that ignited a fire within her. Witnessing the discrimination faced by the transgender community in accessing healthcare, she knew her calling lay in bridging the gap between stigma and service. Driven by a deep-seated empathy and a thirst for knowledge, she pursued medicine, defying societal norms and etching her name in the annals of inclusivity.Dr. Ranjita's impact extends far beyond the confines of her clinic. She is a beacon of hope for the transgender community, offering culturally sensitive healthcare while challenging entrenched prejudices within the medical fraternity. Her clinic is a safe haven, not just for medical treatment, but also for acceptance and understanding.

But Dr. Ranjita's fight extends beyond individual consultations. She actively advocates for policy changes that ensure equal access to healthcare for transgender individuals. She works with hospitals and medical colleges, sensitizing healthcare professionals about gender identity and dismantling harmful stereotypes. Her voice resounds in conferences and seminars, demanding inclusion and advocating for LGBTQ+ healthcare rights.

However, Dr. Ranjita's journey hasn't been without its challenges. Discrimination lingers in the corridors of hospitals and sometimes even in the minds of her patients. Funding for LGBTQ+ healthcare remains limited, and the fight for legal recognition and full healthcare coverage for the transgender community is an ongoing battle.Yet, Dr. Ranjita remains undeterred. Her spirit burns bright, fuelled by the countless lives she has touched, the trust she has earned, and the unwavering belief in a future where medical care is not bound by biases, but by the universal right to health and dignity.

She is a pioneer, a champion for equality, and a testament to the transformative power of compassion. As she continues to wield her scalpel of inclusivity, she reminds us that true healing lies not just in mending bodies, but in mending hearts, dismantling discrimination, and creating a healthcare system that embraces every individual, regardless of their background or identity.

32. Seeds of Change - Cultivating a Future of Inclusivity

In the sun-drenched fields of rural India, where the rhythm of life beats in tandem with the seasons, Manorama Sharma's story blooms like a vibrant sunflower, defying the shadows of prejudice and nurturing a harvest of self-sufficiency for her transgender community. As a farmer and agricultural leader, she doesn't just cultivate crops; she cultivates hope, resilience, and a future where transgender individuals can thrive on their own land, tilling not just the soil, but also the walls of discrimination that have long held them back.

Born in a small village in Haryana, Manorama's childhood was a tapestry woven with whispered anxieties and societal expectations that clashed with her burgeoning identity. Yet, amidst the whispers, her love for the land and its bounty flourished. She found solace and purpose in the rhythm of the seasons, the earthy scent of freshly turned soil, and the quiet satisfaction of a bountiful harvest.

In 2007, Manorama transitioned, a decision that ignited a fire in her soul. Witnessing the struggles of her community, ostracized from land ownership and denied access to agricultural resources, she knew her calling lay in empowering them to claim their rightful place in the fields.Thus began her journey as a pioneer for transgender self-sufficiency in agriculture. She formed the Samata Farmer's Cooperative, a haven for transgender individuals, offering them access to land, training in sustainable farming practices, and a network of support and solidarity.

Manorama's leadership is legendary. She teaches her community organic farming techniques, soil conservation methods, and water management practices, ensuring their farms not only survive but thrive. She negotiates with village elders, challenges discriminatory land ownership policies, and advocates for fair access to agricultural resources.But Manorama's impact extends far beyond the borders of her cooperative. She conducts workshops and training sessions across the state, empowering other transgender individuals to embrace agriculture as a path to self-sufficiency and dignity. She is a vocal advocate for transgender land rights, her voice resonating in government offices, conferences, and media platforms.

However, Manorama's journey isn't without its challenges. Societal prejudice and discrimination continue to cast long shadows, often hindering access to land and resources. Government policies remain inadequate, and funding for initiatives like Samata is often limited.Yet, Manorama remains undeterred. Her spirit, like the sun that warms her crops, shines bright with unwavering resolve. She continues to fight for her community, her hands calloused from tilling the land and her heart brimming with the resilience of a thousand sunflowers.

Manorama Sharma is more than just a farmer; she is a symbol of empowerment, a beacon of hope, and a testament to the transformative power of self-sufficiency. As she continues to nurture not just crops but dreams, she reminds us that true progress lies not just in policy changes, but in the fertile ground of community, in the unwavering belief in one's own potential, and in the quiet dignity of harvesting a life lived on one's own terms.

33. Transgender Odyssey through Film and Theatre

In the luminous realm of Indian cinema and theatre, where stories unfurl on celluloid and stage, Radhika Menon's journey blazes a trail of defiance and artistry. As a transgender actress and director, she doesn't just tell stories; she shatters stereotypes, challenges narratives, and illuminates the marginalized experiences of the transgender community through the mesmerizing prism of film and theatre.

Born Ravi in a small village in Kerala, India, Radhika's childhood was a tapestry woven with conflicting threads. While her spirit revealed in the magic of storytelling and performance, societal expectations and rigid norms cast long shadows. Yet, amidst the whispers and prejudices, an ember of artistic passion flickered within her, refusing to be extinguished.

In 2005, Radhika embraced her true identity, a momentous decision that ignited a fire within her soul. Witnessing the misrepresentation and exclusion of transgender narratives in mainstream media, she knew her calling lay in reclaiming the power of storytelling. Thus began her odyssey through the world of film and theatre, not as a passive observer, but as a creator, director, and actor, determined to rewrite the script.Radhika's film debut in Deepa Mehta's acclaimed "Leela" was a powerful statement. Her portrayal of a transgender woman navigating societal complexities resonated with audiences across the globe, challenging entrenched preconceptions and sparking conversations about acceptance and inclusivity.

But Radhika's impact extends far beyond the silver screen. She is a force to be reckoned with on the theatre stage, directing and performing in thought-provoking plays that tackle themes of identity, discrimination, and the resilience of the human spirit. Her play "The Truth Within," a poignant exploration of her own journey, has garnered critical acclaim and ignited meaningful dialogues about the transgender experience.However, Radhika's path isn't paved with rose petals. Prejudice and discrimination continue to cast shadows, often limiting access to funding, opportunities, and mainstream recognition. The fight for equal representation and casting opportunities for transgender artists remains an ongoing battle, demanding constant vigilance and unwavering determination.

Yet, Radhika remains undeterred. Her spirit burns bright, fuelled by the stories she tells, the lives she touches, and the unwavering belief in a world where art transcends boundaries and embraces diversity. She continues to mentor aspiring transgender artists, her platform becoming a launchpad for marginalized voices to be heard and stories to be told.Radhika Menon is more than just an actress or a director; she is a cultural icon, a voice for the voiceless, and a testament to the transformative power of art. As she continues to challenge narratives and rewrite the script, her journey becomes a beacon of hope, reminding us that true progress lies not just in entertainment, but in dismantling prejudice, amplifying marginalized voices, and creating a world where everyone, regardless of their background or identity, has the right to take center stage and tell their own story.

34. Words Woven from Silence

In the vast library of Indian literature, where ink dances across canvas and whispers become stories, Meera Mahadevi's voice resonates with a unique rhythm. As a transgender writer and poet, she doesn't just craft words; she weaves tapestries of experience, giving voice to the joys, struggles, and vibrant tapestry of the often-silenced transgender community.

Born as Manish in the dusty plains of Rajasthan, Meera's childhood was a landscape of unspoken questions and societal expectations that clashed with her burgeoning identity. Yet, amidst the whispers and anxieties, a refuge emerged – the solace of language, the magic of stories that could capture the essence of who she truly was.

In 2007, Meera embraced her true identity, a pivotal moment that ignited a fire within her. Witnessing the lack of representation and understanding of the transgender experience in mainstream literature, she knew her calling lay in filling the void with her own words. Thus began her journey as a writer, her pen becoming a powerful tool for self-expression and community advocacy.Meera's poems pulsate with raw emotions, delving into the complexities of navigating a world that often seeks to exclude. She writes of the longing for acceptance, the sting of discrimination, and the quiet resilience of the transgender spirit. Her verses paint vivid portraits of lives lived on the margins, celebrating their unique joys and vulnerabilities with unflinching honesty.

But Meera's impact extends beyond her poetry. She is a storyteller, weaving narratives that transport readers into the inner lives of transgender individuals. Her short stories explore themes of identity, love, loss, and the search for belonging, offering poignant insights into the human experience beyond the confines of societal labels.However, Meera's journey isn't without its challenges. Prejudice and discrimination continue to cast long shadows, often limiting access to publishing opportunities and mainstream recognition. The fight for the inclusion of transgender narratives in literary curriculums and mainstream media remains an ongoing battle, demanding constant vigilance and unwavering determination.

Yet, Meera remains undeterred. Her spirit, like a burning ember, refuses to be extinguished. She continues to mentor aspiring transgender writers, her platform becoming a launchpad for marginalizedvoices to be heard and stories to be told.Meera Mahadevi is more than just a writer; she is a cultural icon, a voice for the voiceless, and a testament to the transformative power of literature. As she continues to weave words that challenge stereotypes and celebrate diversity, her inkwell becomes a beacon of hope, reminding us that true progress lies not just in turning pages, but in dismantling prejudice, amplifying marginalized voices, and creating a world where everyone, regardless of their background or identity, has the right to write their own story and share it with the world.

35. A Serve for Change

Natasha, a name synonymous with grace and grit, is not your average athlete. Hailing from the bustling city of Delhi, she has carved a unique path in the world of sports, not just for her exceptional volleyball skills, but for being a transgender woman who is actively breaking down barriers and promoting inclusivity.

Born into a society steeped in traditional norms, Natasha's journey was far from ordinary. From a young age, she felt a dissonance between her assigned gender and her inner identity. Despite facing societal stigma and discrimination, her passion for volleyball remained undimmed. It was on the volleyball court that she found solace, her athletic prowess blooming under the watchful eyes of dedicated coaches.However, the path to competitive volleyball was fraught with challenges. The existing policies and regulations in the sporting arena were not equipped to handle transgender athletes, leaving Natasha in a grey area. Undeterred, she channelled her frustration into determination, advocating for her right to compete and challenging the discriminatory practices that excluded her from her passion.

Her fight for inclusivity resonated with many, and soon, Natasha became a beacon of hope for the transgender community. Her story, one of resilience and unwavering spirit, garnered national attention. Media outlets documented her struggles and triumphs, raising awareness about the plight of transgender athletes and the need for fair and equitable treatment in sports.Gradually, the tide began to turn. Sport's governing bodies started revising their policies, acknowledging the existence and rights of transgender athletes. Natasha's relentless pursuit of justice paved the way for others like her, opening doors to a world that was once closed off.

But Natasha's impact goes beyond policy changes. As a coach, she is a role model for aspiring athletes, encouraging them to embrace their individuality and defy societal expectations. Her training sessions are not just about perfecting spikes and serves; they are also about fostering a sense of community and belonging, where differences are celebrated and everyone feels accepted.On the court, Natasha is a force to be reckoned with. Her powerful smashes and lightning-fast reflexes leave opponents awestruck. But her true victory lies in the way she challenges stereotypes and inspires others. Her every move is a testament to the indomitable human spirit, proving that talent and passion can triumph over prejudice.

Natasha's story is still being written, each victory adding a new chapter to her remarkable journey. She is not just an athlete or a coach; she is a symbol of hope, a testament to the power of inclusivity, and a champion for the rights of transgender individuals not just in sports but in all walks of life. As she continues to soar high, her story serves as a reminder that with unwavering determination and a supportive community, even the most formidable barriers can be shattered, one spike at a time.

36. Challenging the Status Quo

Priya's journey is a testament to the unyielding human spirit, a phoenix rising from the ashes of societal bias and legal marginalization. As a transgender woman and lawyer, she stands at the forefront of the fight for legal recognition and justice for the transgender community in India.Born into a world that often struggles to understand and accept gender fluidity, Priya's early life was marked by a constant struggle against societal norms. The dissonance between her assigned gender and her inner identity cast a long shadow, yet it was this very struggle that ignited her passion for law.

Priya saw firsthand the legal hurdles and discriminatory practices faced by the transgender community, from denial of basic rights like education and healthcare to rampant discrimination in employment and housing. Witnessing the injustice ignited a fire within her, a burning desire to use the law as a tool for change.Her journey to legal practice was far from easy. Law schools, steeped in tradition and often ill-equipped to handle the nuances of transgender identities, presented their own set of challenges. But Priya persevered, her determination fuelled by a deep-seated belief in the power of law to create a more just and equitable society.

Once equipped with the legal arsenal, Priya set out to dismantle the discriminatory walls brick by brick. She fought landmark cases, challenging archaic laws and advocating for legal recognition of transgender identities. Her courtroom victories, each a hard-won battle against prejudice, have paved the way for greater rights and protections for the transgender community.But Priya's impact extends far beyond the courtroom. She is a prolific author, weaving her legal expertise with personal narratives in powerful books that illuminate the lived experiences of transgender individuals. Her words resonate with readers, fostering empathy and understanding, and shattering the stereotypes that fuel discrimination.

Priya is also a sought-after speaker, captivating audiences with her eloquence and unwavering conviction. She travels across the country, engaging in dialogues with policymakers, community leaders, and the public at large, challenging misconceptions and advocating for legislative reforms.Her tireless efforts have earned her recognition as a leading voice for the transgender community in India. Priya has received numerous awards for her work, including the prestigious 'Champion of Change' award from the Ministry of Social Justice and Empowerment.

But for Priya, the greatest reward is the smile on the face of a transgender youth who can now access education, the joy of a community finally recognized and protected by the law, the hope for a future where discrimination is a relic of the past.Priya's story is a beacon of hope, a testament to the power of one individual to make a difference. It is a call to action for all of us to stand up against injustice and create a world where everyone, regardless of gender identity, can live with dignity and respect.As Priya continues her fight, her voice ringing loud and clear, one can't help but feel a surge of optimism. For in her unwavering spirit and relentless pursuit of justice, we see a glimpse of a brighter future, a future where the phoenix truly takes flight, soaring high above the ashes of discrimination.

37. Culinary Journey Beyond Gender Walls

Nestled amongst the bustling spice markets of Delhi, Maya's kitchen hums with an intoxicating symphony of sizzling aromas and clanging pans. Here, amidst the rhythmic chaos, culinary magic unfolds, not just on the stovetop, but in the very essence of the chef herself. Maya, a transgender woman renowned for her vibrant restaurant and infectious enthusiasm, is a living testament to the transformative power of passion, inclusivity, and a good pinch of turmeric.

Born into a society that often struggles to comprehend the fluidity of gender identity, Maya's early life was a delicate dance between her inner self and societal expectations. Cooking, however, became her refuge, a canvas where she could express her vibrant spirit and boundless creativity. Each dish, a poem penned with fragrant spices and fiery chilies, told a story of her struggles, triumphs, and unwavering love for her heritage.Yet, the path to culinary stardom was paved with prejudice and doubt. Navigating the male-dominated world of professional kitchens, Maya faced discrimination and scepticism head-on. But her spirit, like the ginger she loved to grate, was strong and pungent. Undeterred, she honed her skills, her talent blossoming under the tutelage of seasoned chefs who recognized the brilliance simmering beneath the societal stigma.

One day, Maya took a leap of faith. With a fistful of dreams and a suitcase full of inherited recipes, she opened her own restaurant, a vibrant space adorned with splashes of colour and the intoxicating aroma of slow-cooked curries. Here, gender norms were as fluid as the ghee swirling in her dal makhani, and every dish held a story of resilience and reinvention.Maya's culinary creations are not mere meals; they are vibrant tapestries woven with the threads of her identity and experiences. Her menu, a kaleidoscope of regional Indian flavours, celebrates diversity on a plate. Each bite, a burst of unexpected textures and tastes, transports you to a bustling street market in Kerala, a quiet temple kitchen in Tamil Nadu, or Maya's own childhood memories, lovingly translated into edible poetry.

But Maya's impact extends far beyond the four walls of her restaurant. She is a beacon of hope and inspiration for aspiring transgender entrepreneurs, demonstrating that passion and perseverance can overcome any obstacle. Through workshops and mentoring programs, she empowers others to follow their culinary dreams, shattering stereotypes and proving that kitchens, like societies, thrive on diversity.Maya's story is a testament to the transformative power of food. It is a story of defying societal norms, celebrating individuality, and finding solace and expression in the rhythm of the kitchen. As she continues to weave her culinary magic, dish by fragrant dish, Maya paints a future where inclusivity simmers on every stovetop, and acceptance is the secret ingredient to a more delicious and equitable world.

If you find yourself craving a taste of India, step into Maya's kitchen. Let the symphony of spices guide you, and savour not just the flavours, but the story of a woman who dared to dream, cook, and create a world where everyone has a seat at the table. For in Maya's vibrant culinary kaleidoscope, you'll find not just a delicious meal, but a celebration of diversity, a testament to the human spirit's unwavering resilience, and a hopeful vision for a future seasoned with acceptance and inclusion.

38. Weaving Acceptance through Cinema and Community

Rani, a name synonymous with artistic audacity and unwavering empathy, is a force to be reckoned with in the Indian film industry. But her story transcends the silver screen, spilling into the vibrant tapestry of social activism and community building. As a transgender filmmaker and founder of the Mitr Trust, Rani is not just creating art; she is wielding it as a powerful tool to shatter stereotypes, build bridges of understanding, and champion the rights of the transgender community.

Born into a society steeped in traditional norms, Rani's journey was far from ordinary. The dissonance between her assigned gender and her inner identity cast a long shadow, yet it was this very struggle that ignited her creative fire. Finding solace in the world of storytelling, Rani discovered an outlet for her emotions, a way to express her lived experiences and challenge societal perceptions.

As she delved deeper into the world of filmmaking, Rani realized the immense power of cinema to spark empathy and understanding. Her films, infused with raw emotion and poignant narratives, became windows into the lives of transgender individuals, shattering the stereotypes and misconceptions that often shroud their identities.One of her most impactful films, "Mitr: A Friend," tells the story of a transgender woman navigating the complexities of family, relationships, and self-acceptance. The film, lauded for its authenticity and sensitive portrayal, resonated deeply with audiences, sparking conversations about inclusivity and challenging existing societal biases.

Beyond the silver screen, Rani's impact extends through the Mitr Trust, an organization she founded to empower and support the transgender community. The Trust provides educational opportunities, vocational training, and access to healthcare, aiming to create a safe space for individuals to thrive and flourish.Rani's tireless efforts have earned her recognition as a leading advocate for the transgender community. She has received numerous awards for her films and social work, including the prestigious National Film Award for Best Feature Film on Social Issues.

But for Rani, the greatest reward is the smile on the face of a transgender youth who can now access education, the joy of a community finally recognized and respected, the hope for a future where acceptance is not a privilege, but a fundamental right.Rani's story is a testament to the transformative power of art and activism. It is a call to action for all of us to stand up against discrimination and create a world where everyone, regardless of gender identity, can live with dignity and respect.

As Rani continues her fight, her voice ringing loud and clear, one can't help but feel a surge of optimism. For in her unwavering spirit and relentless pursuit of justice, we see a glimpse of a brighter future, a future where cinema becomes a bridge between communities, and acceptance becomes the ultimate cinematic masterpiece.

39. Building Bridges of Inclusivity - Unlocking Potential

Nisha's story isn't woven with silk and silver threads, but with the grit and resilience of a woman who has navigated the labyrinth of transgender exclusion and emerged a radiant beacon of hope. In the bustling heart of Delhi, she founded the Transgender Resource Center, a haven where education and advocacy empower individuals to claim their rightful place in society.

Born into a world that often struggles to understand the fluidity of gender identity, Nisha's childhood was a constant dance between her inner self and societal expectations. Yet, she refused to be confined by the suffocating walls of prejudice. Education, she realized, was the key to unlocking doors and dispelling the shadows of ignorance.Her pursuit of knowledge was paved with challenges. Schools, steeped in traditional norms and ill-equipped to handle transgender students, were often hostile environments. But Nisha persevered, fuelled by an unyielding determination to learn and empower herself.

As her thirst for knowledge grew, so did her awareness of the systemic inequalities face by the transgender community. The lack of access to education, healthcare, and basic rights painted a bleak picture of social exclusion. This realization ignited a fire within Nisha, a burning desire to create a space where information and support would empower her community to thrive.Thus, the Transgender Resource Center was born. It became more than just a building; it became a sanctuary, a vibrant tapestry of learning, legal aid, and community building. Nisha, a natural leader, transformed into a mentor, guiding individuals through the labyrinthine legal system, battling discriminatory policies, and fighting for their right to education and employment.

Her fight wasn't confined to the walls of the Center. Nisha became a familiar face at conferences and rallies, her voice ringing loud and clear as she challenged societal misconceptions and advocated for policy reforms. She spoke not just of statistics and legalities, but of lived experiences, of the hopes and dreams of a community yearning for acceptance.Her tireless efforts bore fruit. The Center flourished, becoming a lifeline for countless individuals. Nisha's advocacy resonated with policymakers, leading to the formulation of more inclusive policies and a gradual shift in societal attitudes.But Nisha's work goes beyond policy changes and legal victories. She is a champion of self-acceptance, encouraging individuals to embrace their identities and challenge the stigma that surrounds them. Workshops on self-care and mental health empower individuals to navigate the emotional complexities of their journeys.

Nisha's story is not just hers; it is a testament to the collective strength and resilience of the transgender community. It is a story of defying stereotypes, of carving a path towards acceptance through education and advocacy. It is a story that reminds us that even the most intricate labyrinths can be illuminated by the unwavering spirit of a single, determined woman.As Nisha continues her fight, her voice a beacon of hope, we see a glimpse of a brighter future. A future where education paves the path to inclusion, where policies embrace diversity, and where acceptance reigns supreme. A future where the Transgender Resource Center, under Nisha's unwavering leadership, continues to illuminate the path for generations to come, reminding us that even in the darkest corners, a single spark can ignite a revolution of acceptance.

40. Rainbow Getaways - A Journey of Inclusivity

Amidst the cacophony of bustling Indian streets, Utsava's travel agency is a sanctuary of quiet purpose. Tucked away in a sun-dappled corner of Jaipur, it's not just a business; it's a portal, a gateway to experiences crafted with empathy and understanding, designed specifically for the often-marginalized transgender community. Utsava, its founder, is a pioneer, charting uncharted journeys not just for her clients, but for inclusivity and acceptance in the tourism industry.

Born into a society steeped in traditional narratives, Utsava's story is one of navigating societal barriers with unwavering resilience. From a young age, she felt the dissonance between her assigned gender and her inner identity. But instead of succumbing to societal pressures, she found solace in travel, devouring travelogues and dreaming of exploring the world beyond the confines of her small town.

As she grew older, the travel bug turned into a burning ambition. However, the reality of a world built for cisgender individuals soon collided with Utsava's aspirations. Discrimination and harassment at travel agencies and tourist destinations forced her to confront the harsh truth – the world of travel wasn't welcoming to someone like her.But Utsava refused to be deterred. Her dream of exploring the world ignited a new fire within her – the desire to create a space where others like her could travel without fear or judgment. And so, in 2014, "Travel Yatri," India's first transgender-owned travel agency, was born.

Travel Yatri is more than just a booking platform; it's a community. Utsava handpicks destinations and experiences that are sensitive to the needs of the transgender community. Cultural homestays replace faceless hotels, local guides replace impersonal tours, and immersive experiences replace sanitized sightseeing. Each journey is curated with care, ensuring that clients can explore unfamiliar terrains while feeling safe and accepted.

Utsava's impact extends beyond her clients. She is a vocal advocate for inclusivity in the tourism industry, organizing workshops and training sessions for hoteliers, tour operators, and government officials. Her voice, laced with personal experience and unwavering passion, challenges age-old biases and redefines the concept of responsible tourism.Her achievements haven't gone unnoticed. Utsava has received numerous awards and accolades, including the prestigious Nari Shakti Puraskar from the President of India. But for her, the greatest reward is the joy in her clients' eyes as they return from their journeys, empowered and brimming with stories of acceptance and self-discovery.

Utsava's story is a testament to the transformative power of travel and the indomitable human spirit. It is a story of defying discrimination, building bridges, and proving that inclusivity is not just a buzzword, but a journey worth taking. As she continues to chart uncharted territories, Utsava's legacy paves the way for a future where travel is not just an escape, but a celebration of difference, a world where every journey begins with acceptance and ends with a profound sense of belonging.So, the next time you dream of exploring the world, remember Utsava, the woman who dared to dream bigger, not just for herself, but for an entire community. For in her journeys, we glimpse not just exotic landscapes, but the boundless possibilities of an inclusive future, where every path leads to acceptance and every travelogue whispers a tale of empowerment.

41. Voice for Amplifying the Unheard

In the bustling newsrooms of India, amidst the clatter of keyboards and the hum of deadlines, Priyanka's voice rings out, clear and unwavering. Not just because of her crisp pronunciation and captivating delivery, but because it represents a seismic shift in the landscape of Indian media – the voice of a transgender woman, a pioneering news anchor shattering glass ceilings and rewriting the narrative of media representation.

Priyanka's journey is a testament to the power of defiance and the unrelenting pursuit of dreams. Born into a society where the concept of gender fluidity often faces ostracization and prejudice, she faced her share of challenges. But Priyanka, like a seasoned journalist, refused to be silenced. She pursued her passion for news with unwavering determination, honing her skills and dreaming of a day when her voice would not just inform, but also inspire.That day arrived in 2014, when Priyanka became the first transgender woman to anchor a news bulletin in India. It was a moment etched in history, a beacon of hope for the transgender community and a resounding challenge to the entrenched norms of media representation.

Yet, Priyanka's fight wasn't over. She navigated the choppy waters of a media landscape often ill-equipped to handle the complexities of transgender identity. Misconceptions and prejudices lurked around every corner, but Priyanka faced them head-on, using her platform to educate and advocate for visibility.Her news segments weren't just about reporting the latest headlines; they were about humanizing the transgender experience. She tackled sensitive issues like discrimination, violence, and lack of access to healthcare, giving voice to a community often relegated to the shadows of society.But Priyanka's impact extends beyond the newsroom. She is a sought-after speaker, her voice resonating at conferences and seminars, challenging stereotypes and advocating for media reforms that ensure fair and respectful representation of the transgender community.

She has also embraced the power of social media, using platforms like Twitter and Instagram to connect with young transgender individuals, offering them a role model and a source of inspiration. Her journey, documented in interviews and documentaries, has become a beacon of hope for countless individuals who dream of breaking free from societal constraints and carving their own paths.Priyanka's accolades are numerous, from prestigious awards to international recognition. Yet, for her, the greatest reward is the change she witnesses, the shift in public perception, the increasing awareness and acceptance of the transgender community.

Her story is a powerful reminder that representation matters. It has the power to challenge assumptions, dismantle stereotypes, and pave the way for a more inclusive and equitable world. As Priyanka continues to break through the glass screen, one headline at a time, she offers a glimpse into a future where diverse voices are amplified, prejudices are shattered, and the media landscape reflects the vibrant tapestry of human experience. From the next time you tune in to the news, listen not just to the words, but to the voice behind them. For in Priyanka's unwavering spirit, in her commitment to truth and justice, we find a testament to the power of one voice to change the narrative, rewrite history, and illuminate the path towards a brighter future where everyone has a story to tell and a platform to share it.

42. Trans-forming Tech

In the sterile hum of silicon labs and the rhythmic clatter of coding keyboards, a quiet revolution is brewing, fuelled by the passion and determination of Anjali. As India's first openly transgender engineer and a staunch advocate for STEM education amongst marginalized communities, Anjali is rewriting the narrative, proving that brilliance blooms in the most unexpected gardens, regardless of societal biases.Her journey is a testament to resilience etched against a backdrop of prejudice. Born into a world that often equates technical prowess with traditional masculinity, Anjali faced constant scepticism and doubt. From her early schooling to navigating the male-dominated world of engineering, she encountered hurdles at every turn. Yet, her love for innovation and problem-solving never faltered.

The world of code became her refuge, a space where logic reigned supreme and creativity soared beyond the limitations of societal expectations. As she mastered algorithms and built intricate circuits, Anjali discovered a sense of belonging she had never known before. Each line of code became a brick paving the path to self-acceptance and breaking down the walls of prejudice.But Anjali's success wasn't solely for personal liberation. It became a beacon of hope for countless young trans individuals who saw a reflection of their own dreams in her achievements. Realizing the dearth of role models and support systems for LGBTQ+ communities within STEM fields, Anjali decided to create them herself.

She founded "Spectrum Coders," a non-profit organization focused on mentoring and training transgender youth for careers in science, technology, engineering, and mathematics. Through workshops, hackathons, and scholarship programs, she provides not just technical skills but also a vital support network, a safe space where young minds can blossom without fear of judgment.

Anjali's impact extends beyond her organization. She is a sought-after speaker at conferences and workshops, her voice ringing loud against the stereotypes that discourage LGBTQ+ participation in STEM fields. She challenges industry giants to create more inclusive work environments and advocates for diversity policies that empower marginalized communities.Her efforts haven't gone unnoticed. Anjali has received numerous awards for her advocacy and technical expertise, but for her, the greatest reward is the sparkle in the eyes of a young trans student who writes their first line of code or presents their innovative project with newfound confidence.

Anjali's story is a powerful reminder that dreams don't discriminate. It's a call to action for educational institutions and the tech industry to dismantle barriers and create opportunities for all, regardless of gender identity. As she continues to inspire and empower the next generation of STEM trailblazers, Anjali's legacy lies not just in the circuits she builds, but in the bridges, she constructs between communities, paving the way for a future where inclusivity and innovation converge to create a brighter, more technological world.So, the next time you marvel at the sleek lines of a new gadget or the seamless navigation of a virtual world, remember Anjali's story. Remember that brilliance can spark anywhere, fuelled by passion, nurtured by support, and unleashed by the unwavering spirit of those who dare to redefine their own narratives. For in Anjali's journey, we witness not just a technical revolution, but a human one, fuelled by the quiet hum of acceptance and the vibrant spark of dreams reaching for the stars.

43. The Lawyer Advocating for Change

In the hallowed halls of Indian courts, where justice often wears blindfolds, Priya Pillai's voice rings out with a clarity that pierces through prejudice and illuminates the long-shadows of discrimination faced by the transgender community. A transgender lawyer and founder of the Transgender Legal Forum, Priya isn't just arguing cases; she is waging a battle for legal recognition, social justice, and dismantling the very pillars of inequality that have marginalized her community for centuries. Her journey is a testament to resilience forged in the fires of adversity. Born into a society steeped in rigid gender norms, Priya's childhood was a constant dance between her true identity and societal expectations. Yet, she found solace in the pursuit of knowledge, her mind drawn to the intricate web of legal codes and the promise of justice they held.

This passion led her to law school, where she faced not just academic challenges but also the sting of discrimination. But Priya refused to be silenced. She navigated the legal landscape with unwavering determination, fuelled by a desire to fight for the rights of a community denied access to basic legal protections. After graduating, Priya faced the brutal reality of a legal system often blind to the struggles of transgender individuals. But instead of succumbing to the apathy, she created her own path. In 2003, she founded the Transgender Legal Forum, a beacon of hope for a community yearning for legal recognition and justice.

Priya's fight is multifaceted. She tackles everything from discriminatory inheritance laws to lack of access to healthcare, from hate crimes against transgender individuals to the fight for legal recognition of their gender identity. Her courtroom victories become milestones in the long march towards equality, each judgment chipping away at the edifice of prejudice. But Priya's impact extends beyond the courtroom. She is a relentless advocate, her voice resonating in government forums, demanding policy changes and legislative reforms that protect and empower the transgender community. She educates the public, dispelling myths and stereotypes through workshops, seminars, and media appearances.

Her work has earned her national and international recognition. Awards and accolades adorn her mantle, but the greatest reward for Priya is the transformation she witnesses in the lives of her clients. Seeing them secure their rightful inheritance, access healthcare, or simply walk down the street without fear is a testament to the power of her legal activism and the unwavering spirit of her community.However, Priya's fight is far from over. The shadows of discrimination still linger, and the path to complete equality remains long and arduous. But with every court victory, every policy change, and every heart and mind she opens, Priya builds a brighter future for transgender individuals.Her story is not just about legal wins; it's about human rights, about dignity, and about the inherent right of every individual to live authentically and freely. It's a call to action for all of us to dismantle the walls of prejudice, to stand in solidarity with the marginalized, and to ensure that in the legal landscape of India, justice truly is blind, not just to colour, but also to gender identity.

As Priya continues her battle for legal and social justice, her voice becomes a chorus, echoing the collective aspirations of the transgender community. It is a reminder that even the most entrenched legal structures can crumble under the relentless pursuit of equality, and that the law, when wielded with passion and conviction, can become a powerful tool for social change.So, the next time you hear the whispers of discrimination, remember Priya Pillai. Remember the woman who dared to defy the status quo, who challenged the very fabric of legal inequality, and who proved that even in the face of injustice, hope can be found in the courtroom, in the streets, and in the unwavering spirit of a community united in its quest for acceptance and equality.

44. Healing the Invisible Scars

In the bustling heart of Mumbai, where life often moves at a breathless pace, Shubhangi's quiet sanctuary offers a haven of solace and support. A transgender psychologist and counsellor, she is not just mending minds; she is weaving a tapestry of well-being, thread by thread, for the marginalized transgender community.

Shubhangi's journey is one of self-discovery and empathy etched against a backdrop of societal stigma and discrimination. Navigating the complexities of her own gender identity in a world that often struggles to understand, she found solace in the realm of psychology.This passion for understanding the human mind led her to pursue a career in counselling. But the path was not without its challenges. Transgender individuals, often facing social ostracization and lack of access to mental health resources, were largely absent in the mainstream field of psychology. Yet, Shubhangi refused to be deterred.

She carved her own niche, specializing in transgender mental health. Armed with her clinical expertise and a deep understanding of the unique challenges faced by her community, Shubhangi became a beacon of hope for those struggling with anxiety, depression, and the trauma of discrimination. Her counselling sessions are not just about clinical assessments and diagnoses; they are conversations laced with empathy and understanding. She creates a safe space where individuals can shed the masks they wear for the world and confront their vulnerabilities without fear of judgment.

Shubhangi's work extends beyond individual therapy. She conducts workshops and seminars, educating both the transgender community and mainstream society about mental health issues and the importance of seeking help. She advocates for better mental health services for transgender individuals, pushing for inclusivity in policies and practices.Her impact has been profound. Countless individuals have found solace in her counselling, their anxieties eased and their self-esteem strengthened. Her workshops have sparked conversations, breaking down barriers and fostering empathy within the community and beyond.

Shubhangi's work has garnered national recognition. She has been awarded for her contributions to transgender mental health and lauded as a champion for LGBTQ+ rights. But, for Shubhangi, the greatest reward is the transformation she witnesses in her clients. Seeing them reclaim their narratives, navigate life's challenges with newfound confidence, and embrace their authentic selves, that is the fuel that keeps her going.

Shubhangi's story is a powerful reminder that mental health is not just a medical concern; it is intricately woven with the fabric of our social realities. It is a call for inclusivity and understanding, a plea for acknowledging the unique challenges faced by marginalized communities. As Shubhangi continues to weave her tapestry of well-being, her work reverberates far beyond the confines of her counselling room. It echoes in the hearts and minds of those she touches, reminding us that true healing comes not just from medication and therapy, but also from acceptance, empathy, and the unwavering belief that everyone deserves to thrive, regardless of their gender identity.

So, the next time you hear the whispers of mental health struggles within the transgender community, remember Shubhangi. Remember the woman who dared to challenge the status quo, who built a sanctuary of support where healing could blossom, and who reminds us that every thread, every conversation, every act of empathy, can contribute to a tapestry of well-being, woven with inclusivity and respect, for all.

45. A Chisel for Change

In the echoing halls of galleries, where light dances on sculpted forms, Shivananda's art speaks volumes. A transgender sculptor and artist, she doesn't just mold clay and bronze; she challenges societal norms, celebrates diversity, and gives voice to the often-unheard narratives of the transgender community.

Shivananda's journey is a tapestry woven with threads of struggle and resilience. Born into a society that often confines individuals within the rigid boxes of gender expectations, she faced the constant sting of prejudice and discrimination. Yet, Shivananda found solace in the world of art, her hands finding a language where words often faltered.

Clay and metal became her companions, their formlessness echoing the fluidity of her own identity. As she sculpted, she gave form to the emotions that society often tried to silence – the longing for acceptance, the defiance against stereotypes, and the vibrant tapestry of experiences that make up the transgender identity.

Shivananda's sculptures are not mere representations of bodies; they are stories etched in bronze and clay. Her figures defy conventional notions of beauty, their limbs reaching out in a dance of self-discovery, their faces etched with the quiet strength of overcoming adversity. Her art is a mirror held up to society, reflecting not just physical forms, but the complex inner landscapes of the marginalized.But Shivananda's impact transcends the gallery walls. She uses her art to engage in dialogues, to break down barriers of ignorance and prejudice. Her workshops and installations become interactive spaces where communities gather, share stories, and celebrate the beauty of diversity.

Her work has garnered national and international recognition. She has exhibited in prestigious galleries, been invited to speak at conferences, and received awards for her contributions to art and

LGBTQ+ activism.However, for Shivananda, the greatest reward is the spark of understanding she ignites in her viewers. Seeing the walls of prejudice crumble in the face of her art, witnessing empathy blossom in the eyes of strangers, that is the true currency of her success.

Shivananda's story is not just about artistic brilliance; it's about using art as a tool for social change. It's a testament to the power of creativity to challenge norms, rewrite narratives, and pave the way for a more inclusive world.As Shivananda continues to sculpt her vision of acceptance, her legacy echoes far beyond the confines of the gallery. It resonates in the hearts and minds of those she touches, reminding us that art is not just a luxury, but a powerful weapon against discrimination, a celebration of human diversity, and a bridge towards a future where every individual, regardless of their gender identity, can find their story etched in the canvas of society, not ostracized to the margins.

So, the next time you stand before one of Shivananda's sculptures, remember the hands that moulded it, not just the form it embodies. Remember the woman who dared to challenge the status quo, who gave voice to the silenced, and who used art to sculpt a world where every identity can find its rightful place, not under the chisel of prejudice, but under the gentle hand of acceptance and celebration.

46. Framing Narratives

In the flickering light of a projector screen, where shadows dance and stories unfold, Arundhati Devi Chandrasekhar paints her vision of the world. An acclaimed transgender filmmaker, she is not just capturing moments on celluloid; she is reframing narratives, reflecting marginalized realities, and amplifying voices long silenced.

Arundhati's journey is a testament to the transformative power of storytelling. Born into a society steeped in traditional norms, she encountered the harsh realities of discrimination and prejudice early on. Yet, she found solace in the world of cinema, its ability to transport her to different realities, to offer glimpses into lives beyond her own.This fascination with storytelling blossomed into a passion. Arundhati devoured documentaries, her mind drawn to the raw authenticity, the unfiltered truths that resonated with her own experiences. But she soon realized that the stories on screen rarely reflected the struggles of the transgender community, a community often relegated to the periphery of narratives.

This realization sparked a fire within her. Arundhati decided to become the storyteller she craved to see. She picked up a camera, her lens becoming a weapon against invisibility, a tool to amplify the voices of her community.Her debut documentary, "Beyond the Binary," was a watershed moment. It delved into the lives of transgender individuals, not as victims of discrimination, but as complex, vibrant beings navigating the world with resilience and hope. The film challenged stereotypes, fostered empathy, and sparked conversations about transgender rights and inclusion.

Since then, Arundhati has crafted a powerful body of work, each film a testament to her unwavering commitment to social justice. She has explored the struggles of transgender youth in "Rainbow Dreams," documented the fight for legal recognition in "The Transgender Bill," and showcased the resilience of transgender entrepreneurs in "Breaking

Barriers."Her films are not just visual narratives; they are immersive experiences. Arundhati weaves in personal anecdotes, historical context, and expert opinions, creating a tapestry of understanding that transcends cultural and geographical boundaries.

Arundhati's impact extends far beyond the screen. Her documentaries have been screened at prestigious film festivals, won international awards, and sparked policy changes and social movements. She has become a vocal advocate for transgender rights, using her platform to educate audiences, challenge prejudices, and advocate for legislative reforms.Her work has garnered international recognition. She has been featured in leading publications, invited to speak at global conferences, and awarded prestigious fellowships for her contributions to documentary filmmaking and LGBTQ+ advocacy.

But for Arundhati, the greatest reward is the impact she has on her viewers. Seeing tears of recognition in the eyes of transgender individuals, witnessing minds open to new perspectives, that is the true currency of her success.Arundhati's story is not just about personal triumph; it's about reclaiming the power of storytelling. It's a testament to the potential of film to bridge cultural divides, spark empathy, and champion social justice.

As Arundhati continues to weave her narratives, her camera capturing the struggles and triumphs of the marginalized, her legacy echoes far beyond the film festival circuit. It reverberates in the hearts and minds of those she touches, reminding us that stories have the power to change hearts, dismantle prejudice, and ultimately, create a world where everyone, regardless of gender identity, can find their voice and be seen, heard, and celebrated.So, the next time you hear the click of a camera capturing a story often ignored, remember Arundhati. Remember the woman who dared to hold up a mirror to society, who reframed narratives with a lens of empathy, and who proved that documentary filmmaking can be more than entertainment; it can be a powerful tool for social change, a catalyst for a more inclusive and just world.

47. Rebooting Diversity

In the bustling silicon valleys, where lines of code dance like constellations on screens, Nitasha's journey is a beacon of inspiration. A transgender software engineer and tech entrepreneur, she is not just writing algorithms; she is rewriting the narrative of transgender inclusion in the tech space.

Born into a society that often pigeonholes individuals based on gender norms, Nitasha's childhood was a constant struggle against societal expectations. Yet, she found solace in the world of numbers and logic, her mind drawn to the intricate puzzles of coding and the endless possibilities of technology.

This passion led her to pursue computer science, a field often dominated by stereotypes and limited opportunities for transgender individuals. But Nitasha refused to be deterred. She navigated the challenges with unwavering determination, her resilience fuelled by a desire to prove that talent and passion, not gender, define success in tech.After graduating with honours, Nitasha faced the harsh reality of discrimination in the job market. Companies, blinded by prejudice, failed to recognize the brilliance hidden beneath her transgender identity. Yet, Nitasha refused to be discouraged. She honed her skills, taking on freelance projects and building her portfolio, proving her mettle with every line of code she wrote.

Finally, her talent and perseverance paid off. Nitasha landed a coveted position at a leading tech company, becoming one of the first openly transgender engineers in her field. Her success shattered the glass ceiling, opening doors for other transgender individuals who had long felt ostracized from the tech space.But Nitasha's impact extends far beyond her own career. She is a vocal advocate for STEM education and inclusion, inspiring young transgender individuals to pursue their dreams in technical fields. She visits schools and colleges, sharing her story and debunking myths about the tech industry being a closed door for LGBTQ+ individuals.

Nitasha's workshops are not just about coding; they are about empowering young minds to break free from stereotypes and embrace their full potential. She teaches them not just algorithms, but also resilience, self-belief, and the importance of advocating for themselves.Her work has garnered national and international recognition. She has been featured in prestigious publications, invited to speak at conferences, and awarded for her contributions to STEM education and LGBTQ+ rights.

But for Nitasha, the greatest reward is seeing the spark of passion ignite in the eyes of young transgender students. Seeing them overcome their doubts and embrace the world of technology with confidence is a testament to the power of her advocacy and the transformative potential of STEM education.Nitasha's story is a powerful reminder that the tech world, like any other field, thrives on diversity. It is a call to break down barriers, dismantle stereotypes, and create a space where talent and passion are celebrated, regardless of gender identity.

As Nitasha continues to code a path to inclusion, paving the way for future generations of transgender engineers and tech entrepreneurs, her legacy goes beyond the screen. It echoes in the hearts and minds of those she inspires, reminding them that the only limit to their dreams is the one they set for themselves.So, the next time you see a line of code dancing on a screen, remember Nitasha. Remember the woman who dared to break the mold, who challenged the status quo, and who proved that in the world of technology, the only thing that matters is the magic woven by your mind, not the labels society tries to impose.

48. Breaking Chains-Winning Rights

In the hallowed halls of justice, where logic reigns and arguments clash, Ashita's voice rings with the clarity of a clarion call. A transgender lawyer and legal aid provider, she is not just wielding legal expertise; she is carving a path towards equality, brick by legal brick, for the marginalized transgender community.

Ashita's journey is one of resilience etched against a backdrop of legal and societal discrimination. Born into a society that often struggles to comprehend identities beyond the binary, she faced ostracization and prejudice from a young age. Yet, Ashita refused to be silenced. She found solace in the pursuit of knowledge, devouring legal texts like they held the key to unlocking justice.

This passion for law led her to pursue a career in advocacy. But the path wasn't smooth. Discrimination followed her into the courtroom, with judges questioning her very right to practice law and clients hesitant to entrust their legal battles to a transgender woman. Yet, Ashita persevered, her spirit fuelled by a deep-seated desire to dismantle the legal barriers that ostracized and marginalized her community.She built her practice on the foundation of compassion and understanding. Ashita's clients weren't just case files; they were individuals with stories, struggles, and a desperate need for justice. She tackled discrimination in employment, housing, and healthcare, challenging discriminatory laws and fighting for equal access to basic rights.

But Ashita's reach extends beyond individual cases. She is a fierce advocate for systemic change, pushing for policy reforms and legislative amendments that protect the rights of transgender individuals. She lobbies for anti-discrimination laws, works with policymakers to draft inclusive legislation, and challenges biased interpretations of existing laws.Her courtroom victories are milestones in the long march towards equality. From securing legal recognition for transgender identity to upholding the right to self-determination in healthcare, Ashita's legal battles set precedents and pave the way for a more just and inclusive future.

But Ashita's impact goes beyond landmark judgements; she instils hope. Seeing marginalized individuals empowered to claim their rights, watching fear replaced by confidence – that is the true reward that fuels her fight.Her work has garnered national and international recognition. She has been awarded fellowships, invited to speak at global forums, and lauded as a champion of human rights and LGBTQ+ equality.

However, for Ashita, the truest reward lies in the impact she has on the lives of her clients. Seeing the spark of hope in their eyes, witnessing them reclaim their rights and dignity, that is the fuel that keeps her fighting.Ashita's story is not just about legal victories; it's about dismantling societal and legal barriers. It's about proving that the law, when wielded with courage and compassion, can be a powerful tool for social change.But Ashita's fight is far from over. Discrimination still lurks in the shadows, and the road to complete equality remains long and winding. Yet, with every legal battle won, every policy change advocated for, and every voice amplified, Ashita's legacy continues to grow, paving the way for a future where the scales of justice are balanced, not by prejudice, but by the inherent dignity of every human being, regardless of their gender identity.

As Ashita continues to fight for her community, her voice, echoing with the voices of countless individuals, reminds us that true justice cannot be confined within the walls of a courtroom. It demands a societal transformation, a dismantling of harmful stereotypes, and a celebration of the diverse tapestry of human experience. In Ashita's unwavering spirit, we see a glimmer of hope, a promise that one day, the law will truly serve all, and the scales of justice will tilt towards equality, not just for the privileged few, but for every member of the human family, regardless of their gender identity.

49. Embracing the Spectrum of Beauty

Beneath the glittering spotlights, where silk whispers and sequins shimmer, Priyo strides with the defiant grace of a revolution. A transgender model and fashion designer, she isn't just gracing the catwalk; she is challenging norms, rewriting narratives, and carving a space for LGBTQ+ visibility in the often-monolithic world of fashion.

Priyo's journey is a testament to the transformative power of self-expression. Born into a society that often suffocates identities that stray from the binary, she faced the harsh realities of discrimination and invisibility from a young age. Yet, instead of succumbing to societal pressures, Priyo embraced her uniqueness, finding solace in the transformative world of fashion.Clothes, for Priyo, were not just fabrics and trends; they were a language, a way to articulate her vibrant internal world. She experimented, defied traditional labels, and embraced fluidity in her personal style, each daring outfit a silent rebellion against societal expectations.

This passion for self-expression led her to the world of modelling. But the fashion industry, like most other realms, was not ready for Priyo's unapologetic defiance of gender norms. Casting agents dismissed her, designers hesitated, and the runway seemed an insurmountable distance away.Yet, Priyo refused to be silenced. She created her own platform, using social media to showcase her unique style and challenge conventional beauty standards. Her bold photoshoots, her eloquent posts about LGBTQ+ rights, and her infectious confidence resonated with audiences worldwide.Fashion magazines started noticing, designers began collaborating, and soon, Priyo found herself walking the very runways that had once rejected her. But Priyo wasn't just another model; she was a catalyst for change. Her presence on the catwalk, her fierce strut, and her defiant gaze shattered stereotypes and sparked conversations about inclusivity and diversity in the fashion world.

Beyond modelling, Priyo has carved her own path as a fashion designer. Her label is a bold celebration of LGBTQ+ identities, a rejection of binary constraints, and a vibrant tapestry of self-expression. Her designs are not just clothes; they are statements, wearable affirmations of individuality and a call for celebrating the spectrum of human experience.Priyo's impact extends far beyond the catwalk and the fashion magazines. She is a vocal advocate for LGBTQ+ rights, using her platform to raise awareness, challenge discrimination, and empower marginalized communities. She speaks at conferences, works with LGBTQ+ organizations, and uses her voice to dismantle harmful stereotypes and bridge the gap between the fashion industry and the LGBTQ+ community.Her work has garnered international recognition. She has been featured in prestigious publications, awarded for her contributions to LGBTQ+ fashion, and hailed as a champion of inclusivity and diversity.But for Priyo, the greatest reward lies in the impact she has on her audience. Seeing young LGBTQ+ individuals find confidence in their own identities, seeing society's perception of beauty shift to encompass diversity, that is the true currency of her success.

Priyo's story is not just about personal triumph; it's about reclaiming the power of self-expression. It's a testament to the transformative potential of fashion and the undeniable beauty of defying norms.As Priyo continues to strut her defiance on the catwalk, her bold designs adorning bodies that refuse to be categorized, her legacy echoes far beyond the glittering lights. It reverberates in the hearts and minds of those she inspires, reminding us that fashion, like any medium, has the power to spark change, celebrate individuality, and ultimately, create a world where everyone, regardless of gender identity, can walk the runway of life with confidence and pride.

So, the next time you see a model who defies traditional norms, remember Priyo. Remember the woman who dared to walk a path less travelled, who made fashion a platform for change, and who proved that true beauty lies not in conformity, but in the vibrant tapestry of self-expression, regardless of the label's society tries to impose.

50. Words Ignite Change

In the hushed silence of ink-stained pages, where words dance and emotions bleed onto the canvas of verse, Nisha's voice echoes with the thunder of a thousand unheard stories. A transgender poet and activist, she isn't just weaving words; she is weaving a tapestry of resilience, amplifying the voices of marginalized communities, and fighting for a world where poetry becomes a weapon against injustice.

Nisha's journey is a testament to the transformative power of language. Born into a society that often silences voices that don't conform, she faced the harsh realities of discrimination and prejudice from a young age. Yet, Nisha found solace in the whispering embrace of words, in the way they could capture the complexities of her identity and the injustices she witnessed.

Poetry became her shield and her sword. She wrote of the sting of rejection, the ache of societal expectations, and the burning desire for acceptance. Her verses, raw and unflinching, resonated with other marginalized individuals, their shared struggles finding solace in the rhythm of her words.But Nisha's poetry wasn't just about personal catharsis; it was a call to action. She used her platform to speak out against discrimination, to challenge societal norms, and to advocate for the rights of transgender individuals and other marginalized communities. Her poems became rallying cries, igniting conversations about equality, justice, and the inherent dignity of every human being.

Nisha's impact extends far beyond the pages of her book. She is a vocal advocate for LGBTQ+ rights, environmental justice, and social welfare. She organizes workshops and slam poetry events, empowering young people from marginalized communities to use their voices and fight for their rights.Her work has garnered international recognition. She has been featured in prestigious literary magazines, invited to speak at conferences and rallies worldwide, and awarded for her contributions to social activism and LGBTQ+ literature.But for Nisha, the greatest reward lies in the eyes of a young transgender person who finds solace in her words, in the spark of hope ignited by a poem, in the realization that they are not alone.

Nisha's story is not just about literary prowess; it's about giving voice to the voiceless. It's a testament to the power of poetry to transcend boundaries, challenge norms, and ultimately, create a world where everyone, regardless of gender identity, background, or belief system, can find their voice and their place in the vibrant tapestry of humanity.

As Nisha continues to weave her poems, her words echoing in the streets and resonating in hearts, her legacy echoes far beyond the literary circles. It reverberates in the lives of those she touches, reminding us that poetry is not just about aesthetics; it is a tool for social change, a weapon against injustice, and a beacon of hope in the darkest of times.So, the next time you encounter a poem that speaks to your soul, remember Nisha. Remember the woman who dared to wield words like weapons, who made poetry a platform for activism, and who proved that language, when used with passion and purpose, can truly change the world, one verse at a time.

###

About Author

Ajit Kumar is an empathetic and inquisitive individual who is always looking for ways to connect with the world around him. He believes that everyone has something to offer, and he is passionate about using his skills and talents to make a positive impact on society.

He has done double master's in History one from Nalanda University and IGNOU. He earned his bachelor's degree in history from Atma Ram Sanatan Dharma College, University of Delhi. He was also selected for the Gandhi Fellowship, where he worked on a variety of projects related to heritage and education. He writes numerous research papers which was selected in national and international conferences and published by renowned publications in a form of chapters.

Presently, Ajit is working as a content writer in the corporate sector, but he also runs a blogging website with his friend. He is interested in a wide range of topics, including inner-peace, mysticism, history and culture.